TRUSTING HIM IN YOUR GRIEF
Encouragement for Grieving Parents

TRUSTING HIM IN YOUR GRIEF
Encouragement for Grieving Parents

TABLE OF CONTENTS

By Charlotte Holt

By Charlotte Holt

Comments and Prayer
By Charlotte Holt

About the Author

Foreword
By Lisa Ludwig

Grief is an undeniable part of human existence. From the day Adam and Eve sinned, grief has been intertwined with the joys, the triumphs, the victories, and the defeats of everyday living. But is endurance all there is to be gained from having suffered? Are the lessons taught simply those of learning to move on after the death of a loved one? Or is there more?

Wrapped in the pages of this book are the testimonies from mothers and fathers who have learned what it means to trust God in the midst of deepest sorrow. Nestled in each tale are the heartache of unimaginable loss, and the wondrous triumph of ultimate healing.

With courage and compassion, Charlotte Holt has compiled a bouquet of testimonies and prayers that is sure to minister to the hearts of those stricken by grief. Her wisdom and insight that follow each tale provide both blessing and encouragement, while the prayers act as a soothing balm to those with scars, either old or new.

May you be blessed by the reading of this book, and may the grace of God touch you as you read and experience the outpouring of the Father's miraculous love.

Introduction

Are you grieving? If not, you will. Grief is something every person must face at one time or another. We all have occasion to grieve in our erratic journey through life. We do not all handle our grief the same. However, certain stages and steps designed by our Creator helps us through the grieving process, regardless of the type of loss we face.

Whether the loss of a child, grandchild, relative, spouse, friend, loved one, acquaintance, marriage, or a job, grief must be dealt with and overcome.

I have mediated upon this process many times. Now I am ready to put something into written form. Experiencing multiple losses in my life, I feel the time has arrived to share my greatest grief with others. By demonstrating the ways in which God brought me through, I hope to help others relate, learn or be encouraged by what I write.

When thinking upon this venture, I realized God loves others as much as he does me, even though I find this concept hard to comprehend. Therefore, I wanted to include other's testimonies of God's grace through their grieving time as well. I knew if He brought me through,

He helped others also. Like the old hymn says, "What He's done for others, He'll do for you."

Think about this. Many people die in this world. Each and every one is someone's child. If the parents have not preceded them in death, this leaves hurting parents. Therefore, innumerable persons lose their child or children.

Grieving the loss of a child never ends, but continues throughout one's life. Though different stages come, parents never get over the loss, for losing a child is unnatural. We expect our children to bury us, not the other way around.

The people whose stories I've used here know the God of the universe.

Therefore, they hold a special key to help others in their grief. That key being: trust in the One who made them and redeemed them. They have grown stronger, not only in spite of, but because of their grief. Therefore, I have named my book, *Trusting Him in Your Grief - Encouragement for Parents Losing a Child*. Hopefully, it will help parents to trust Him and to overcome in the midst of their grief.

But we do not want you to be uninformed, brethren, about those who are asleep, so that you will

not grieve as do the rest who have no hope. 1
Thessalonians 4:13 (NASB)

I pray that as others read this book, they will come to know their Heavenly Father more. If they do not know Him, they can. Thus, everyone can have this hope. They must only invite Him into their heart. He surely will come if He's asked in earnest.

I want to begin by sharing this poem God gave

me when I grieved for my sons:

Grieving
By Charlotte Holt

When you grieve for someone you love,
Call upon your Father above.
He'll be there any day or hour.
Rely on His great power.

No matter what the day may bring,
He's the one who makes the Robin sing.
He'll wipe away every tear from your eye.
He'll save them in a bottle when you cry.

He's a friend who sticks closer than a brother.
A friend like Him, there is no other.
He'll see you through your darkest night.
Tomorrow He'll make the sun shine bright.

If you rely on Him, He'll make you proud.
He'll bring you out of the dreary cloud.
When you mourn for your precious loss,
He'll pick you up and wipe away the dross.

He'll make you stronger than you were before.
He'll say, "My child, what are you grieving for?
Don't you know I'll handle him with care?
And all your burdens, I'll share.

One day you'll see him again face to face
When you come to live in my Heavenly place.
Don't you understand he was only on loan?
Heaven is his true home.

Trusting Him In Your Grief/Charlotte Holt

I gave him to you for just a while,
He came to make your
heart smile.
Don't be sad, my friend.
It will all work out in the end.

Keep on keeping on, until I come.
Run your race, until it's won.
Your loved one's here with me.
Your loved one has been set free.

Please don't worry or frown.
Your loved one now wears a victor's crown.
You must continue to carry on
'til you're called to your Heavenly home.

Then with your loved one, you'll always be.
His face you'll forever see.
Please don't worry and fret.
My precious one, your time hasn't arrived yet.

Just lean on me whenever you're down.
Be reminded of your victor's crown.
A few more stars you must earn,
Before you make Heaven your home.

Let your heart be comforted and still.
Continue to walk in my perfect will.
Don't be downcast and sad,
I'll be with you and make you glad.

Go on with your life and don't look back.
I'll go with you and you'll not lack.
Your loved one's happy here with me.
Please let him go and set him free.

Trusting Him In Your Grief/Charlotte Holt

In the process you'll be free.
You'll live your life more abundantly!
I give you these truths, so you may know
I'll always be with you, wherever you go."

Dedication

It only seems logical to dedicate this book to my two sons, Louis and John, at least in part. I am thankful the Lord gave them to me for a few years. They blessed my life in more ways than I can ever say in my short testimonies. They helped the Master form my life and mold me into the image I see today.

However, I would be remiss if I did not also dedicate this book to each child represented here and the parents who bared their heart and told their stories.

May the Lord bless each of them, their families, friends and also all those who come behind with a loss of their own, through this book   May pleasant memories of each lost loved one remain as we release them to God and His care. Giving them over to Him demonstrates the best way we can trust Him in our grief.

I, also, would like to dedicate this book to the memory of Barbara Johnson. She planned to endorse it but went home to be with Jesus before I found a publisher. She first inspired me with her book, *Splashes of Joy in the Cesspool of Life,* when I traveled some hard roads with my sons. Even though, I've always loved to write, her writings inspired me on my own journey.

When I wrote her about endorsing the book, she called right away and agreed to do so. She said, "I know this book will help and encourage many people." My prayer is that her words were prophetic.

Acknowledgements

So many people have made this book possible and I want to acknowledge them all, starting with my great and awesome God, who prompted me to begin this book even when I didn't know how. I put my faith and trust in Him, and He has seen me through. At times when I thought, I don't know if I can do this, He whispered in my ear, "Yes, you can in My strength." Both of us knew I couldn't do it alone and on my own.

He used several people to help guide, lead and direct me. He sent my friends and critique partners to play their part in helping me – Sharen, Janice and Nancy – thank you so very much. Sharen directed me to the right people to contact in regard to my author release and other information. She referred me to Marlene Bagnull, who I can't thank enough, for her contribution and advice.

Janice encouraged, guided and taught me numerous things about the writing process. Nancy gave me names and organizations to contact, encouraged and helped as well.

Also, Sally Stuart and Kathleen Y'Barbo helped with their copyright and legal advice. Marcia Gruver, a friend and fellow writer, encouraged me all along the way.

Lisa Ludwig, one of the story contributors and author of the foreword, answered my prayer to help with the editing of the book. I will be forever grateful to her. I couldn't have done it without you, Lisa.

Denise McEwen line edited for me after the manuscript was completed. I am so grateful to her and appreciate the help. Bless you, Denise.

Several of the contributors for this book also read and edited. Thank you all. You know who you are.

My precious, husband, Charles, I always want to acknowledge. He stands behind me, encourages me, reads my stuff, accompanies me to book signings and speaking engagements on occasion, allows me to go to writers' conferences, and continues to be my best support system other than my Savior. I tell him almost daily, "You're my favorite person in the whole world." And he is. Thank you, my dear, Charles. I couldn't have done any of it without you.

Most importantly, they all prayed for me and supported me.

Chapter One
He Gave His Only-Begotten Son
By Anne Bryan Westrick

When I saw the proposed title of this book –
Trusting Him in Your Grief – I shook my head. Trust?
That sounded so easy, when grief wasn't easy at all. I
had a lot to say about grieving, but the word trust didn't
come to mind. Before writing about the Lord being with
me in my grief, I'd have to tell you how I thought He
wasn't there. How alone I felt. How isolated and angry.
For me to write about the loss of my child, I'd have to
tell you how low I sank before I felt Him lift me up.

The sinking started the day I went to my
doctor's office for a routine second trimester check-up.
The doctor kept frowning and moving the stethoscope
across my swollen belly, trying to hear the heartbeat.
Eventually, he said, "Let's do a sonogram today."

We watched the monitor as a little form
appeared through the fuzziness – a human form, too
small to fill the screen. Little arms and hands, legs and
feet, the beginnings of a face. A perfect baby. Dead.
Lying on the floor of my womb, on her back,
motionless.

"I'm so sorry," the doctor said. "I'll schedule a D&C, remove the fetus, and let your body heal." (D&C means Dilation and Curettage, a medical procedure to open the cervix and gently scrape out the womb.)

"What if you don't do the D&C?" I asked. My question really meant: What if the sonogram is wrong? What if she's still alive?

"If I don't do it, you'll cramp up eventually and your body will expel the fetus."

I shook my head. "No, don't schedule anything," I whispered. I went numb. A white noise like a loud refrigerator pulsed through my ears. Colors dimmed. The world became very small.

Driving home, I told myself, concentrate; keep your mind on the road. I went to the grocery store and shuffled up and down the aisles, clutching the cart for balance. I shuddered. There's a dead baby inside me. I am a walking graveyard. A cemetery strolling between shoppers, and nobody knows it. No one, but me.

My husband consoled me through the next two days. My body did nothing. I prayed and read the Bible, but found no comfort. Years earlier I'd gone to seminary for a Master's degree. I studied grief and its stages. I knew I was denying the death of this child, but I couldn't

25

help it. Intellectually, I told myself I had faith and my faith would see me through, but emotionally I was incapable of feeling it. I was incapable of feeling anything. I went through each day in a fog.

When I couldn't stand any more waiting, I asked the doctor to do the D&C. He scheduled two more sonograms, just to make sure. My husband and lots of medical personnel saw the dead baby on the monitor, too. Then I took the anesthesia, woke up medically cleansed, and went home.

I couldn't sleep. I tried, but I lay there, staring at the shadows, listening to the night. About four in the morning, I took a shower and started crying. I cried like I'd never cried before. A deep cry. A wailing. A weeping and gnashing of teeth. I threw my head backward into the pulsing water, begging this nightmare to wash itself away.

Not only was my womb empty, but also my soul. I felt abandoned. Maybe there was no God. After years of Bible studies, prayer groups and worship, what had ever made me think that He existed at all? I felt so totally, hopelessly alone that I thought my earlier faith-filled years had been a delusion.

In the following months my husband and I dealt

with the loss differently. He needed to talk about it less and I needed to talk more. I prayed with my pastor. I went to a Compassionate Friends meeting. I spoke with friends, but my fog only grew thicker. When I saw dead raccoons on the highway, I burst into tears. I read the obituaries. I pulled out my concordance and looked up every Bible passage about women wailing, women crying over the loss of their children, women mourning. I was one of them, but there was no obituary for my baby, no funeral, no public recognition of my loss. I felt guilty that I cried for a daughter who had never been born when so many parents cried for children they held and kissed. I told myself their pain was worse than mine, but that only made my guilt stronger. I felt selfish crying over a condition society shrugs away as a common miscarriage, but I couldn't stop the tears.

"This is what it means to be human – this pain. This grief," I mumbled one day while pacing my bedroom floor. "How dare you, God. How dare you put us here to experience this pain. This excruciating, life-numbing hollowness. This unbearable suffering. How dare you create such an awful, imperfect world."

He came like a rustling in the curtains, a pulse in the rocking chair. From the corner of the room, He whispered, "It's okay. You can be angry with me. Go ahead. Tell me how angry you are. I can take it."

I yelled at Him. I threw His book at Him. "You are so terrible. You give us this capacity to love, then take away from us what we love the most!"

"Tell me about it. I know. I lost a son." He said. And I thought I heard Him cry.

"You stopped existing," I said. "I wanted to believe in you, but I couldn't. You left me."

"I've been sitting by your side for months now, rocking in your rocking chair, listening to your grief, waiting for you to acknowledge me." He said quietly. "You've been rambling and ranting and stewing. You thought you were alone, but you weren't."

I sat down and breathed again for the first time since the miscarriage-long, deep breaths of fresh air. For months I'd felt as if a mask covered my face. But now- this was oxygen again. I don't remember whether He said it, or exactly how I knew it, but on that day, I was resurrected – I was given new life.

I didn't cry anymore when I saw dead squirrels. I stopped reading the obituaries. I noticed little things like ants marching along the windowsill, and I smiled at the life around me. I knew I would never stop loving or embracing life, even though embracing it meant I could lose it, and the fog might reappear. But I could face the fog now because I wasn't alone.

Six months later I miscarried another child. I cried. We both cried – my husband and me – but this time was different. This time I wasn't angry.

This time I heard a new meaning in that oft-quoted passage: For God so loved the world that He gave His only begotten Son... He didn't give the Garden of Eden, or the oceans, or the mountains, or the birds of the air or the fish of the sea. No, he gave His Son. He understood my grief and He listened to my anger – the anger that had blocked my faith for months. He reached out, held my hand, and whispered, "I know how hard it is to lose a child. I've been there. It's hell. And I'll continue to sit by your side for as long as you need me. For eternity.

A. B. (Anne Bryan) Westrick is the Administrative Director at JamesRiverWriters.org. A graduate of Stanford University and Yale Divinity School, she recently received her MFA in Writing from Vermont College of Fine Arts. Her first novel is forthcoming from Viking/Penguin in the fall of 2013. www.abwestrick.com

Charlotte's Comments

Numbers of women go through the ordeal of miscarriage. At times people look at their grief as less important than giving birth and then losing the child. They think of it as not yet a reality. They are mistaken. This living, breathing child formed inside this mother represents the love between a man and woman. The mother and father not only lose the child the mother carried inside her body for months but they lose their dreams and future plans for and with this child. This loss leaves an empty spot just like the loss of any other child.

If you are a parent who has lost your child in this way, my heart goes out to you. Better still, the heart of God reaches out to you and permeates the deepest creases of yours with His love. If you let Him, He will come inside and heal your heart. Let Him touch your emotions. Let Him cleanse your soul. Let Him revive your spirit.

God knows our every thought. He knows when we harbor anger against Him. So, why not tell him as Anne did. If you have lost a child in this way, or any other way for that matter, tell God how you feel. Let him comfort you and heal your hurt. Remember, he too lost a Son. He not only lost Him. He gave Him for us.

God not only understands. He's there for us in the midst of our pain and grief. Generally, we look to others to meet our needs or help us in our grief. No one can meet those needs or help us the way our Heavenly Father can. If we try to depend on man, we find disappointment, but depending on God never ever fails us.

God may not do things the way we want or even expect, but His ways rise much higher than ours. He gives us what's best for us, often in spite of our agendas and us. He loves us more than we could ever love ourselves or anyone else. Be assured He works things for our good.

I don't believe God ever causes bad things to happen to any of us, but he will take the bad circumstances of our life and work them for our good. He will use whatever we go through to strengthen us for our good and use us to help others.

Prayer: *Lord, help us all to be sensitive to the grief of others. Help us understand when they grieve differently than we do. Help us not keep our focus on ourselves but to meet the needs of those around us. Help us to recognize You are the only one who can see us through our grief. You are the One we can depend on in whatever state we find ourselves. I pray in Jesus Name. Amen.*

Chapter Two
"Deep Waters"
By Catherine B. Bell

In my mind's eye, I see a high mountain meadow carpeted with thick grass. I am there. My baby is with me. We live together in a sunny world apart from others, sharing everything – air, food, water, life. She hears my voice; I feel her kicks. She is growing healthy and strong. My love for her breaks my heart with joy. Hands held high, I bask in the warmth of the favor of the Lord. Elizabeth and I dance and worship before Him.

At the meadow's edge, where green grass cannot grow among a million sharp rocks, a cliff falls into an angry sea. I take one step ... backwards. I tumble headfirst into black crashing water. The sun disappears; darkness descends.

Suddenly, with no warning, everything is changed. "Where am I? What happened? The baby is stillborn? Elizabeth is dead? No! No! No!"

In the midst of fierce winds, I hear a far-away voice explain, "A cord accident. It was wrapped so tight around her neck, the blood supply was cut off."

Waves hit, assaulting ... waves of denial, waves of confusion. I thrash. I fight to breathe. I fight for control. I am going under! *Oh God, God where are You?*

A hand gentle yet forceful, lifts me into a

lifeboat. *He reached down from on high and took hold of me; He drew me out of deep waters.* Psalm 18:16 (NIV)

The lifeboat is the very Word of God, pieced together, a firm and sure refuge. Huddled deep within it, clinging, I am rescued, safe. The storm rages, the waters crash, I feel it all around, but I am saved.

Day after day, the storm continues. Thoughts about Elizabeth are constant. I struggle with God over her death.

"Why, Lord? What was the purpose? I want her back!" I make impossible, unreasonable, illogical bargains with God. "Please, please, please," I beg.

The answer is always, "No."

A phone call comes. "Dad is dying. Come to the hospital."

Another death. Another funeral. So unexpected. The waves pitch and roll the boat. I am sick with sorrow. "Oh God, what's going on? Why this? Why now?"

So many questions…where are the answers? In His Word: *"For I know the plans I have for you,"* *declares the LORD, "plans to prosper you and not to harm you, plans to give you hope and a future. Then you will call upon me and come and pray to me, and I will listen to you. You will seek me and find me when you*

seek me with all your heart. I will be found by you,"
declares the LORD. Jeremiah 29:11-14a (NIV)

I miss my father-in-law, but I am tormented with longing for Elizabeth. I want her back, knowing I can't have her back. *So we let go our hold of things we held very dear. Things that once were counted as gain we now count as loss, and out of what seems emptiness, come beauty and richness.* (Elisabeth Elliot) I choose to stop struggling. I accept Elizabeth's death, force open my hands, and let her go.

Then come waves of crushing sorrow. I accept Elizabeth's death, but now I must accept that I will grieve, and grieving will last a long time. The unrelenting deep sadness, the hot tears, the soul-cry: "God, where are you? I need you! Why are you crushing me?" I cling to the lifeboat, the Word of God. *Those who know your name will trust in you, for you, Lord, have never forsaken those who seek you.* Psalm 9:10 (NIV) I hold on to those words. He has not forsaken me. I will trust Him.

Weeks pass by. The waves continue to build and crash. Waves of anger. Waves of self-pity. I learn to offer them to God as a sacrifice. It's hard to do. I find these emotions are seductive, they feel good, but they offer no comfort, only more distress. Over and over I give them to God and receive his comfort, His peace. *Praise be to God... the Father of compassion, and the God of all comfort, who comforts us in all our troubles.* 2 Corinthians 1:3-4 (NIV)

Because he himself suffered when he was tempted, he is able to help those who are being tempted. (Hebrews 2:18 (NIV)

There are other waves I do not try to fight. Waves of deep profound sadness. I let them wash over me, embracing them. I weep and scream and let myself feel the loss. I learn that trusting God does not take away the pain. I cry out for help. He does not remove my heartache, but he enables me to endure it, and comforts me with His constant presence and the promises in His Word.

I find my lifeboat rides the waves high and low. One day is a good day, relatively calm. Another day is storm-tossed and, like the disciples, I despair. Grief is a terrifying roller-coaster ride.

I find that in the midst of intense pain, there may be moments of quiet joy. I experience this joy in intimate prayer. *You have made known to me the path of life; You fill me with joy in your presence, with eternal pleasures at your right hand.* Psalm 16:11 (NIV)

Months pass by. Still in the lifeboat, still over deep waters, still trusting Him, the pain continues. The water grows calmer. The lifeboat becomes my schoolhouse, with Jesus as my tutor. I learn much in the year that follows. I learn that God runs the world. Nothing happens outside His decree. God is a sparrow watcher. (Matthew 10:29-31)

I learn to forgive others. I expect them to read my mind, know my needs, and meet them. No one can meet my unrealistic expectations. Others disappoint me by staying away or pretending that Elizabeth never existed. *Bear with each other and forgive whatever grievances you may have against one another. Forgive as the Lord forgave you.* Colossian 3:13 (NIV)

I learn that grief is no excuse for sin. Jesus is my example, teaching me how to live with suffering, and live well. *To this you were called, because Christ suffered for you, leaving you an example, that you should follow in his steps. He committed no sin, and no deceit was found in his mouth.* 1 Peter 2:21-22 (NIV) I learn to live with grief, to roll with it, to plumb its depths. I learn to let suffering transform me, make me look more like Jesus. Elizabeth's life was too precious for me to waste this experience, or throw it away as if it were meaningless.

I learn that I have a choice with each new day – to grow bitter or grow better. I choose the latter.

Catherine B. Bell *lives with her family in south-east Pennsylvania. She works in an office cubicle pulling staples and shuffling papers while dreaming of the writing life. Cathy often quotes Ann Lamott's two favorite prayers: "Help me, help me, help me!" and "Thank you, thank you, thank you!"*

Charlotte's Comments

According to the National SUID/SIDS resource center, sudden infant death syndrome (SIDS) was the third leading cause of infant death for 2008 and the first leading cause of death among infants, ages 1–12 months. A total of 2,353 SIDS deaths occurred in 2008. An estimated 26,000 SIDS deaths occur annually in the U. S., many of them at or near full term. Stated another way, 1 in every 115 deliveries is a "still" baby. Despite advances in so many areas of obstetrics, the incidence of stillbirths in many states has been rising in over the past decade.

What anguish these parents must face. They have long awaited the day of their child's birth. A day, which should be one of the happiest of their lives, turns out to be one of the saddest. Their hopes, their dreams, for this child they have longed for and nourished for nine months, now gone.

Like with the miscarriage, family, friends, acquaintances and others sometimes treat this death like it isn't as important or traumatic as that of a child who lives longer. However, for those experiencing this loss of a child hurt the same as any other parent.

They may never hold their child, never feed them, never change their diapers, never watch them crawl, never see them take that first step, never kiss the baby cheek, never experience them cutting the first tooth, never hear them say the first word or never be called Mama or Daddy by them. They will never watch the child grow up to be a man or woman. Never see their child marry and give them grandchildren. In some ways, their loss feels emptier.

God will manage to work this for their good, as He does for any of us. He will give them other blessings. Perhaps, a ministry to others going thorough this potentially devastating time, a heart to reach out to others, an understanding mate and the list could go on. God knows their needs and will supply them. The only condition is for them to allow Him to do so.

If you are a parent who has lost a child in this

manner, know God hurts for you. He wants to heal your heart. He does not want you to grieve forever. His Word says, …Weeping may go on all night, but joy comes with the morning. Psalms 30:5 (NLT)

He wants to give you joy instead of mourning. He wants you to take off your sackcloth. He wants you to dwell on the things that are good and lovely and of good report. He does not want you to continue in your grief. I realize we must grieve to some extent and it is healthy to go through the grieving process and stages. If we get stuck in our grief, we are not turning it over to God and trusting Him in our grief. Remember, we do not grieve as the heathen.

Certainly we will always miss that child. But if we can think on the good things in our life, like the strength He gives us through the process, we can grow spiritually.

I'm not telling you to forget your child. None of us ever will. Nor, am I telling you to cover over your grief. I am saying don't hang on to grief, other people or even your lost child – hang onto God. He will see you through. Get better instead of bitter. Let God turn your mourning into dancing.

Prayer: *Lord, fill our empty arms and hearts. Help us*

*to be sensitive to the needs of others who grieve. Help us
to take off our sackcloth and turn our mourning into
dancing, as you want us to do. Help us to rely on You
and remember we need not grieve as if we didn't know
You. In Jesus Name. Amen.*

Chapter Three
Four Minutes of Life
By Melinda Weidenbenner
As told to Michelle Weidenbenner

"What do you mean our baby doesn't have a brain? How is that possible?" I lay on the examining room table with my bare, protruding abdomen exposed to the chill of the air-conditioned office. The room began to spin, my ears burned and my eyes stung from my tears as I peered into the TV ultrasound screen.

My husband, Mike, our two little boys, and I, had waited for this doctor's appointment all month. The boys were excited to see their new unborn brother for the first time on the ultrasound monitor and hear his swishing heartbeat. Now that I was six months pregnant, he had grown to the point where we could see all his tiny body parts. This was supposed to be a learning experience—a bonding time—for our children. Instead, it became a horrifying dream.

The boys laughed when I pulled my slacks down to expose my belly. I shivered when Doctor Mabee spread the cold KY jelly onto my skin. He put the tiny camera probe in the goop and moved it around.

"Here are his little legs. See the tiny arms?" He pointed out the various body parts letting our children climb closer to the monitor to get a better look. "See his head here?" Then he became silent while he continued to move the probe. It seemed like several minutes lapsed before he finally spoke, looking far too concerned.

My stomach did a somersault as I watched him. I sat up on the table. "What's wrong?"

"Perhaps it would be better if I talked to you and your husband alone." He beckoned to the nurse and asked her to find some stickers for the boys.

"Go ahead. We'll be right here," I said. "You go with the nurse for a few minutes so we can talk to the doctor."

With the nurse's encouragement they left the room. My hands trembled as I waited for the doctor to speak. What could it be?

It was then that he whispered the horrifying news.

"Based on what I see here, it appears that there is a genetic problem with your baby. Do you see his head here?" He pointed to the screen. "The top part of the head is missing. Your baby has anencephaly—which means he never developed a brain."

My heart jumped into my throat. "How can that be?"

Three weeks after conception, a flat strip of tissue along the back of a fetus rolls up to form a tube. The tube develops into the spinal cord, and at one end, the brain. Think of it as a zipper. This neural tube zips up as fast as we zip a zipper. Unfortunately, one little notch didn't close. If the zipper doesn't close all the way, the brain never forms."

"Isn't there anything we can do to close that zipper?"

"No. There never is."

"How will our baby live without a brain?"

"Your baby will die. Many are stillborn. Some live after birth for a few minutes, but there's nothing you can do."

Shocked, I held the sides of my abdomen. "No! This can't be true. I've been healthy. I take my vitamins and eat my vegetables. I don't smoke or drink. Why did this happen?" I didn't want to believe him. He was wrong! My baby kicked all the time. I knew he was alive. Tears filled my eyes as I reached for Mike's hand. "Why?"

The doctor handed me a box of tissues. "There's nothing you've done wrong. You didn't cause this problem, nor could you have prevented it. It's a genetic disposition. I'm sorry. I know this is difficult. If you'd like to get a second opinion I can give you the name of another obstetrician.

"What will he look like when he's born?" Mike asked.

"He'll look normal except for the top of his head. It'll be open and hollow where the brain would have been."

I didn't know what to say. Mike held me as his tear-filled eyes searched my face in an attempt to comfort me. I'd never heard of a baby without a brain. All our hopes and dreams for this child were shattered— just like that.

"What do we do now?" Mike asked.

"We can schedule an appointment for you to deliver the baby next week. We'll induce labor and abort the baby so you won't have to carry it for the remaining term. I'm sorry for this bad news."

I don't remember getting up from the examining table or walking out the door to go home. My boys were concerned when they saw my red face and swollen eyes. After Mike explained the baby's condition to them they were sad, too. "Why can't the doctor operate and put a new brain in his head?" Our six-year-old son asked.

"Doctors can't perform that kind of surgery," I said. "He will die, but its okay. Death is a natural thing. When he dies he'll be in God's hands in heaven."

We went home and prayed for guidance. Something didn't feel right. I couldn't abort this baby. We were opposed to abortion. I needed to consult another physician first. What if our doctor made a mistake? Why did I need to abort this child? Was I in any danger? What risk was I in if I let the baby come in God's time?

Finally, after seeking a second opinion, we got the response we needed. "Yes, your baby has anencephaly, but there's no more risk in carrying him to term than there is carrying a healthy baby to term," the specialist said.

We knew what we had to do. The decision was easy now that we understood I wasn't at risk. I would carry the baby to term. I wanted him to be a part of me for as long as possible because I knew it wouldn't be forever. I cherished the movement within me.

We named him Zane, which means God's grace, and I talked to him every day. *Dear God, please let me have the rest of my time with this child and take him only*

45

when you are ready. I'll not let him go until You say it's time.

For three months my abdomen grew larger. Zane continued to kick and move about. Every day I talked to him as I caressed the skin that kept him safe. I felt sad that Mike couldn't experience the sacred little tingles that clinched my bond.

There were times I prayed for a miracle that our angel would be born healthy. But as the time grew nearer, I began to accept the possibility that this might not happen. Instead, I thanked God for my other children and for dying for my sins. I knew that our pain was far less than what God had endured when He died on the cross. Eventually, I began to pray that our little bundle be born alive—even just a few minutes—so I could hold him in my arms. I waited, as with my other pregnancies, for God to decide his natural birth date.

A week before my due date I went into labor.

"I don't want anything for pain." I told the doctor as I lay on the birthing table. "I want to do this naturally." I secretly hoped that by delivering Zane without drugs it would increase his chances of living for a few minutes.

My dream came true. He was born alive. He didn't cry, but his little arms and legs moved slowly and peacefully. Mike and I both held him and I dressed his sunken head with a warm hat. After we said our good-byes our children were ushered into the room. They each held him, kissed his little hands and feet, and whispered their good-byes, too.

Zane lived for four minutes. Our youngest son held him and said, "He doesn't look bad. He looks like an angel."

The plants and shrubs that we planted during my pregnancy with Zane continue to flourish as a reminder of how he would have grown if things had been different. When I weed and water those plants I am reminded of another time when Zane was a part of me. I'm still thankful for those memories.

Today was Valentine's Day. Just like every holiday, we tried to include Zane's memory in our festivities. We baked heart-shaped cookies, iced them with sugar and red hots and took several to the cemetery where Zane's stone awaited our visits. As we laughed and ate red cookies, I once again thanked God for leading us to our decision to wait for Zane's natural birthday.

In living through the birth of Zane, our children have come to respect life—however short it may be.

Story of Melinda Weidenbenner (as told to her sister-in-law Michelle Weidenbenner)
This article ran on www.kyria.com a part of *Christianity Today.*

Melinda Weidenbenner *lives in southern Indiana with her husband, Mike and two sons, Ryker and Holden. When she's not hanging out with her boys she can be found sewing window treatments, making jewelry, drawing, or praying with a friend.*

Michelle Weidenbenner *is a YA author and blogger at Random Writing Rants, Teaching Adults and Teens How To Get Published. Her current wips include: The Muggler, Willow, Love is Just a Word, Kelly's Story, and The Vision in a Kiss. She's been published in Adoptive Families, Brio Magazine, Church Libraries, Kyria, The Writer's Digest and has won contests in both The Writer's Journal and The Writer's Digest. Diana Flegal from Hartline represents her. Besides writing she's a tennis junkie, a book slut, and a fun-loving Mimi.*

Charlotte's Comments

I greatly admire this couple for their decision not to abort. Even though, the results didn't change, the time they had with their precious baby meant a great deal to all the family. They will always have these precious memories of their child. There is not much I can add to this beautiful story.

Prayer: *Lord, bless this family for their willingness to comfort others through the pain they have experienced. Thank you for the comfort you bring to all of us when we lose a child.*

Chapter Four
"13 Diamonds"
By Nancy C Anderson

My new neighbor touched my hand and said, "What a lovely ring, it looks like an antique. It's so unusual, where did you get it?"

I replied slowly, carefully choosing my words "I had it custom made."

"I have a friend who's a jeweler. Would you mind if I copied it?" She asked.

I smiled, "First, let me tell you the story behind the design."

It was just after New Years Day in 1990 when I found out I was pregnant with our second child. My Husband, Ron, was thrilled, but I was apprehensive. Our five-year-old, Nick, had several learning disabilities and he was quite a "hand-full." I told Ron, "I'm afraid I won't have enough energy to take care of Nick *and* a newborn baby."

I went for all the required check ups and

the doctor assured me that everything was fine. However, since I would be 35 when the baby was born, and that meant I had a higher chance of a baby with birth defects, the doctor wanted to do an ultrasound.

I tried to find a comfortable spot on the hard examination table as the nurse's aid squirted the cold sonogram gel on my expanding belly. One technician slid the scope over my stomach as the other one watched the monitor. I looked at the woman who watched my baby on the screen. Her face didn't have much expression. Then it did. Her eyes widened and her hands flew involuntarily to her mouth as she made a sad squeaking sound.

"What's wrong?" I asked. I sat up and repeated my question.

She tried to compose herself as she scurried toward the door. "I'm sorry." She whispered.

The other technician left too, so I tumbled off the table and went to look at the picture still on the screen. I didn't see anything unusual. It just looked like a blurry negative of a skinny baby. I looked down at my stomach and rubbed it as I whispered a prayer. "Oh Lord, I think we're in trouble. Please help us."

After the amniocentesis, my husband and I went

back to the hospital for the test results. The doctor spoke as if he was reading from a textbook.

"Trisomy 18 is a genetic disorder that always involves profound mental retardation and severe disfigurements." Then, he said the words that still live inside a tiny zipped pocket of my heart. "Your baby's condition is usually incompatible with life. Most women in your position-- in order to spare themselves unnecessary anguish--just get an abortion. We can schedule yours for tomorrow morning."

I wasn't able to speak. I stopped breathing. I felt like I was drowning. I wanted to drift down into the cool dark water and disappear. A silent tear slid down my face and we left the office without a word.

That afternoon, I prayed. "Lord, I believe abortion is wrong, but I don't want to go through 'unnecessary anguish.' On my own, I don't have the strength to fall in love with a baby who is going to die. Please show me how."

As I prayed, I remembered the Lord could have chosen to avoid the horrific anguish of the cross. *What if He had taken the easy way out?* I understood the value of His gift was measured by the greatness of His suffering. I told the Lord, with renewed strength, "I offer my pain to You as a gift. I will not abort this child."

I kept saying it, even before I meant it. "I choose to love this baby with all my heart." I willed my words into actions. In faith, I moved my hands as I timidly caressed my stomach. In faith, I moved my lips as I mouthed the words, "I love you." No sound came out. I kept repeating the phrase until my brain found the secret passageway to my heart and I was free to taste the bittersweet tears of loving a child who would never love me.

"Try not to think about the future," my mother said. "Your baby is alive today-be alive with him. Treasure every moment."

I talked to him, sang lullabies to him, and gave him gentle massages through my skin. I knew that I might have to do my best mothering before he was born. Each day I prayed, "Lord, please let him live long enough to know that he is loved. Let us have time to kiss him hello and kiss him goodbye. Let his life be free of pain and full of love. Please, Lord, give us the strength to bear this unbearable burden."

Four months later, we met little Timmy, face-to-face. The nurse covered his fragile, 20-ounce body, in a soft blue blanket and matching cap. His heart monitor

beeped an unsteady greeting as she handed him to me.
His beautiful little rosebud-mouth surprised me.
It was an oasis of perfection. We held our emotions in
check, knowing we had to pour a lifetime of love into a
minuscule cup. Ron and I took turns rocking him as we
kissed his soft cheek. Repeatedly, we told him, "We love
you, Timmy." He never opened his eyes. He felt no pain.
His heartbeat got slower and slower and then,
reluctantly, stopped.

We kissed him goodbye and introduced him,
through prayer, to his Heavenly Father. "Lord, here is
our son. Thank you for the gift of his precious life and
for the privilege of being his parents. We release him
into your healing arms. Thank you for answering our
prayers. Amen"

Then we cried.

**I looked at my neighbor's tear stained face
and said, "I had this ring made within a few days of
his birth. I drew a picture of what I wanted, told the
jeweler *why* I wanted it and he worked late into the
night to have it for me the next day." She looked
closer as I explained the design. "The ring has two
curved bands of gold. The longer one symbolizes my**

husband's arm and the smaller band represents mine. Our 'arms' are holding a small, lavender alexandrite (Timmy's birthstone).

She was silent for a long time. "You should be the *only* person in the world to wear that ring," she said. "I won't copy it. Tell me about the diamonds."

There are 13 tiny diamonds; one precious jewel for each moment he was alive. I wear it on my 'baby' finger. He's always with me."

For you formed my inward parts, you covered me in my mother's womb. I will praise You, for I am fearfully and wonderfully made. Psalm 139:13-14a (NKJV)

Adapted from *Avoiding the Greener Grass Syndrome* by Nancy C. Anderson. Published in *Avoiding the Greener Grass Syndrome (Kregel 2004), God's Way for Women (Harrison House 2003)* and *God Answers Mom's Prayers (Harvest House 2005).*

Nancy C. Anderson *is an author and speaker, who encourages women to replace their fears with faith and discover the freedom of an abundant life. She is the author of "The 'Greener Grass" Syndrome, Growing Affair-Proof Hedges Around your Marriage" (Kregel Publications 2005) (714) 206-9540 WWW.NancyCAnderson.com NCAwrites@msn.com*

Charlotte's Comments

Another set of parents I applaud for their decision to keep their child and not abort, no matter the outcome. They trusted God not only in their grief but to carry them through the time of waiting, delivery and then loss.

What a beautiful remembrance they share of their child. As I have said repeatedly throughout this book, we will never forget our children. This ring, representing the life span of a child, stands as a testimony to others about God's provision, tender love and care through the hard times, as this beautiful story illustrates.

If you have lost a child, perhaps, some type of remembrance will be of help to you. Seeking God's provision and strength will prove to be the best thing you can do. Then rely on Him and keep a positive attitude in regard to your loss as Nancy shows in her story.

Prayer: *Lord, we thank You for the fond remembrances we have of our children. May we treasure them forever in our heart, whether physical or mental. Help us to release our children to Your loving care and thank You for the time You gave us with them. In Jesus Name. Amen.*

Chapter Five
A Picture of the Heart
By Linda Lufkin

Love filled my heart as I watched my husband holding our newborn son in his arms. He gazed at his tiny form with such warmth and tenderness. As we shared that love, an image was etched on my mind that would become a precious memory. In the wonder of the moment, we were unaware Kevin would be with us for only a few days. Pleasant and sad memories start to emerge as I look back, with new meaning now. These memories were not forgotten but were stored away in my heart.

Del and I had two children when Kevin was born. We enjoyed the first day of excitement on the arrival of our third child. Kevin resembled his brother and sister in so many ways. We marveled as we held him at how God made each of our children with their own identity, yet with a likeness of our family. From the day Kevin was born, his calm and quiet spirit evidenced his gentle personality. Naturally, my affection for him began to grow and I couldn't wait to take him home.

The next day, the nurse told us that the doctor

wanted to talk to us. A look of concern was displayed in the doctor's eyes. "We suspect that your baby has a problem regarding his heart," he said. "We'd like to keep him for a few more days and take some tests, then we'll send him home with a heart monitor." And that was the way we thought it would be.

After answering all of our questions, the doctor reassured us that he'd keep a close watch on Kevin throughout the night. I looked at my baby as he snuggled contently in my arms. I touched his soft cheek, and then handed him to the nurse. She asked if I had noticed a blue hue to his complexion. I had noticed his little features and wisps of platinum blond hair, but only his eyes were blue.

Early the following morning, Del nudged me to wake up. Kevin had to be taken to a heart specialist for a cardiac catheterization. After the results were back the doctor said, "I discovered that the left side of Kevin's heart is abnormal with incomplete valves. The condition is called Hypoplastic Left Heart Syndrome. This is hard for me to tell you but this affects the major side of the heart and there is nothing that can be done to save his life. He has only a few hours left...I'm terribly sorry."

We could hardly believe what was happening.

We looked at each other and our hearts were crushed with anguish. We felt so alone and confused. Right at that moment God had not intended to leave us alone. The heart specialist was like an angel sent to minister to us in our immediate moment of distress. She not only explained the medical situation, but also showed an unusual amount of empathy. We found out later that she had lost a child the same way a year earlier and understood how devastated we felt.

After the doctor left, we called our pastor and he came immediately. His presence was fresh with God's compassionate love. He went to see our baby, and then he stayed with us, prayed and shared several verses from the Bible. I know now that God sustained us through the pastor's love during our time of waiting.

About an hour later, the doctor returned. There was a distinct sadness all around us. I knew...Kevin had gone to be with the Lord.

When I went home, my arms felt as useless and empty as my heart. At the funeral, I stared through clouded eyes at the small white casket, which held my baby whom I would never hold again. Even though I understood that my baby went to heaven, I couldn't deny the tremendous loss I felt. I thought I would never feel normal again.

Depression battled with my perspective on life during the months that followed. I didn't care about anything. Fortunately, God stayed close to my aching heart, and in my despair I turned to His waiting, open arms. I found hope in reading the Bible as I drew closer to Him. I especially found the Psalms to be tranquil medicine to my grieving spirit. God's Word became my consolation. Faithfully, He revealed His presence through the compassionate love of others. Through their prayers, concern and encouragement I was gradually lifted to life again.

We are thankful for the few precious days we shared with Kevin. He will never be forgotten. Since then God has blessed us with two more children. Just like our four other children, Kevin will always be a part of us. The moment of love that my husband and I shared with our baby will always be vivid in my mind. We have his picture to remember
what he looked like, and his memory to keep in our hearts.

Going through this experience has given my life a different meaning. Although the process of sorrow was emotionally painful to endure, it turned out for good so that I may know God "who comforts us in all our

troubles with the comfort we ourselves have received

from God" (2 Corinthians 1:3).

Now my heart reaches out to share the comfort that God
has given me. We were touched in a way we would
never have known if we had not gone through the
experience of losing Kevin. God was there for us. He
knew what we would need in our time of sorrow. He
gave us peace beyond understanding—a peace that
conveys a picture of the heart of God.

Published by Living With Preschoolers, 1992, and Hope
Magazine, 1999 in memory of Kevin Shawn Lufkin June
26, 1977- June 28, 1977.

*Linda Lufkin is married to Del and they have four
grown children and twelve grandchildren. She is the
author of text for mini books for Havoc Publishing,
stories and poems published in Christian magazines and
contributions to her church newsletter. Her first book, A
Pathway to Healing, was published with Xulon Press.*

Charlotte's Comments

Linda, too, found grief hard but reached out to

God in and through it. God sent just the right doctor to

minister to these parents' needs at a crucial point, just as

He will send Linda to others. Fortunately, her Pastor

comforted and consoled the family with the love of God.

God brought Linda through a terrible time of

depression and despair and through His Word He lifted

her up. He did a work of compassion in her heart to

reach out to others in their grief. He brought her through, as she trusted Him, just as He will anyone in her same situation. No, Kevin will never be forgotten, for he will always have a special place in the family's hearts and life – each and every one of them.

Linda learned about the peace of God and strives to pass it on to others. She learned about the important things of life and wants to share them with all going through this process of grief.

Prayer: *Lord, we thank You for all the fond and precious memories You give us of our children. We thank You for the people You send into our paths to help or encourage us. We thank You for the strength You give us to come through this most awful tragedy of losing our child or children. Thank You that we can reach out to You in this time of pain and desperation. Help us to reach out to help those around us in their trials. In Jesus Name. Amen.*

Chapter Six
By Grace Alone
By Shannon McNear

What can you say when people tell you, "You must be so strong," and you know you aren't? Or, "I could never handle having to go through what you did."

There's nothing, except to refer them to God's grace.

God tailor-makes our trials, and equips us to go through them – only ours, no one else's.

July 1999. Duncan Reid was our sixth child and our third home birth. There was no sign of distress until his head was born. Then we found the cord around his neck, too tight to either pull over his head or to clamp and cut. I had to just push, stretching the cord and partially separating the placenta, which compromised his oxygen. When we couldn't get Duncan to breathe, Troy made the call to EMS, who resuscitated and intubated Duncan and transported both of us to the hospital.

Duncan was transferred to the local medical university NNICU. For the next week and a half, we rode a roller coaster of hope and despair—praying, believing God for a miracle, shored up by family and friends. I kept it together, emotionally, while at the hospital with Duncan. But at night the tears flowed as I sat in front of the computer with the emails and message board posts, full of encouragement and empathy.

The day came when we had to turn off the machines. Incredibly, Duncan breathed mostly on his own for three hours before slipping away quietly in his Daddy's arms.

Family members and a close friend gathered with us for an hour or two afterward, weeping and taking turns holding the tiny shell that had been our baby. My husband broke down as he shared the words the Lord had impressed upon him when Duncan winged his flight home.

Thank you.

What were we to make of that? In the eleven and a half days between Duncan's birth and death, we had tried above all to trust the Lord, for whatever lay in store. At one point during the hospital ordeal, I felt that Duncan was not even the one whose life lay in the balance—that this trial of faith was something far greater than whether or not our son would stay with us or go home early. I was but a vessel—a channel for a brief flash of glory.

During that week and a half, we marveled over details that God orchestrated, things that came together in far more than coincidental manner. We continued to see His fingerprints as we made funeral and burial arrangements—a memorial service in one city, where we lived, and burial in the rural community of Troy's childhood. Every penny we spent from the time Duncan was born until after the funeral was covered by gifts. While Troy and I conducted the simple graveside service, he read from Scripture, I sang and unseen hands held us up. Somehow the Lord shone through us in such a way that the funeral director in Troy's hometown refused payment for his services, so touched was he by our display of faith.

Then it was home, and back to real life.

For two weeks, I had been carried. Now I had to learn to walk again . . . to begin by crawling. I was no stranger to grief. My adoptive father died of cancer when I was seventeen, a month after my high-school graduation. About the time I went off to college that fall, I was tired of crying—figured others were as well—so I shut it away. Little did I know that the grief would come spewing out again a year later, violently and inconveniently, and send me into a tailspin of health problems that eventually took me out of college altogether.

This time, I determined to allow myself to grieve properly—whatever that might mean. I knew the grief needed to run its course. I wanted to be able to realize when a wall of sorrow blindsided me, as it often does, that this was part of the process, and accept it, not merely endure it.

In theory, good. In reality . . . something else again.

What constitutes proper grief? I am still not sure. My intellectual needs were seen to—I knew Duncan was "safe in the arms of Jesus," that someday I would go to him, though he could not return to me. In fact, some of my most intense moments came from feeling I had been overlooked, left behind. God plucked a rose for heaven from my growing bouquet, and insisted I stay behind to finish whatever task He had given me to do.

The crawling metaphor is the closest one I could think of. When a person has been wounded, they spend a certain amount of time lying in bed, recuperating, but at some point they have to get up. Stretch unused muscles. Push past the pain to a place of survival. To refuse the process of healing is to lie down and die—and I could not accept this option.

So I went on. And the Lord led me step by agonizing step—through caring for my older children, reminders that I was needed—and ministering to my husband in his own sorrow, even when I didn't feel like being intimate, because I knew he needed it. I was so grateful to find an article, early on, outlining some differences in how men and women grieve. If not for that article, I fear we might have shipwrecked before things settled. The divorce rate for couples that experience this kind of trauma is about 80%.

The older children reflected both our grief and their own. Their reactions ranged between anger, sorrow, and regret for never getting to hold their youngest sibling. (I regret to say we didn't think of asking during their infrequent visits to the NNICU.) I strove for a balance between being open and real in my own grieving and not overly distressing them, but when my emotions felt most out of control, I often thought everyone would be better off without me. Still, I sensed the Lord standing by with compassion and love, letting me cry, scream, even rail at Him. He understood. He, too, walked the road of grief—indeed, "bore our grief" Himself.

Three months after Duncan's home going, I

conceived again. Toddling steps now filled with terror and elation. Sometimes, like that toddler, I'd stop and cry and lift my arms for the Lord to carry me again. Sometimes He did; other times He coaxed me on a few more steps. Above all, He kept me close to Him, even when I wanted to lag behind or go far away from Him.

Nine months after Duncan's death, while I was about six months along with the next baby, my husband entered a new phase of grieving and became short-tempered with all of us. Somehow the Lord helped me see that he was reacting out of his hurt and anger, and not to take offense . . . and once again, we passed through.

A year and two days after we said farewell to Duncan, Cameron came into the world, after an intense birth. The Lord saw us safely through labor and delivery (again, at home, which we felt at peace about, since the circumstances of Duncan's birth were unlikely to occur a second time), and this baby seemed destined to bring sunshine to all our lives.

A new complication presented itself in the second year—a full-blown crisis of faith. It wasn't that I didn't believe God existed, or that He loved me—but I wondered whether He was quite—fair. Why should I pray if He were sovereign and would do whatever He willed anyway? How could I, a mere human on earth, move the inexorable hand of the God of heaven?

Eventually I came through that as well, and slowly gained strength in my prayer life. I'm not quite as reckless as before—maybe a good thing. I have softened toward others who not only are suffering, but experience similar crises of faith.

Almost six years later, the Lord has blessed us with three more babies, each of them a delight. My husband and I are closer than we've ever been. Looking back, I can see that the Lord used this awful time to wake us up to things that needed attention in our relationship. And I am learning, day by day, to better appreciate my children and life in general. Am I perfect? By no means. I still struggle with patience and diligence and . . . everything a mother usually does . . . and whenever someone comments about my strength, I still laugh with surprise, because I know that inside, I'm truly not strong.

It was all from Him.

Shannon McNear and her husband of 25 years are the parents of eight here on earth, one in heaven. They've endured moving halfway across country and several military deployments as well as the loss of a child, so she tries hard to thank God every day for his grace and mercy.

Charlotte's Comments

Shannon definitely experienced the grace of God. How did she find it? She made a choice to trust Him and let Him carry her through this most horrible time. Whenever, we are weak; He is strong. She relied on His strength and He came through for her. He will do the same for any of us.

She recognized her own limitations and accepted what she could not do by herself. God gave her other children to bless her life. He made her marriage stronger than ever before. When parents lose a child, the marriage undergoes a great strain. Sometimes husband and wife blame each other or themselves. The divorce rate is approximately 50% in the United States.

I wonder how many of those marriages split apart due to the loss of a child and its emotional impact on the partners. I was unable to find accurate statistics. Almost everyone I talk to knows at least one couple that has split after the loss of a child. Some tell me the percentage of broken marriages, after the loss of a child, is as high as 80-90%. How this must grieve the Father, who above all wants to heal our broken hearts.

We can learn from Shannon's example to rely

Trusting Him In Your Grief/Charlotte Holt

on His strength to get us through the tough times. We should make a conscious choice to trust Him through all our grief. He will not disappoint us. "I guarantee it!" As some commercials might say.

Prayer: _Lord, how we thank You for Your grace. Help us to recognize our own limitations and rely on You for our strength. Hold us up when we are weak. Help us know how to depend on You in our struggles. Help us to become stronger in our marriages, in ourselves, in our ministry to others and in our times of grief. In Jesus Name. Amen._

Chapter Seven
Our Warrior
By Curtis Mosley

While a young man in the military in North Carolina, my wife of three years became pregnant. We were both excited about having a child and were encouraged by our close circle of Christian friends and our parents. My wife Cheryl took on a glow about her that was obvious to those around her. We never really considered the possibility that anything could be wrong with our child.

Very early one morning, Cheryl's water broke and we hurriedly dressed and drove through the darkness to the hospital. The medical personnel placed Cheryl in a private room and connected her to various electronic monitors. Thus began an agonizing ten hours of labor. I comforted my wife during this time by reading passages in Ecclesiastes and Psalms.

Although a doctor and nurse came by to check on Cheryl early in her labor, we had little contact with attending medical personnel. Supervision of Cheryl's labor was largely left to the machines that occupied the

72

room.

The nurse assigned to the maternity ward made periodic visits to look at the readings displayed by these devices. Unfortunately, the nurse on duty didn't make her rounds in a timely manner and the condition of the unborn baby became critical.

Although this was her first pregnancy, Cheryl's pain became so great she knew something had to be wrong. I left my wife's bedside to locate the nurse and found her reading a book. She reluctantly agreed to come in to check the monitors. Upon seeing the readings, the nurse hysterically whirled about to summon the doctor. Within minutes, doctors prepared to deliver our son by Caesarian section, a surgical opening of the womb.

A stack of 20 or so papers were pushed in front of me to sign allowing the procedure to take place. Within minutes, anesthetics and surgery were administered.

I waited in the hall. In a short while, a nurse scurried past me cradling what seemed to be a bunched up blanket. She did not make eye contact with me as she raced by. No one approached me for what seemed like a long time. I continued to wait alone, my heart anxious

and my thoughts in turmoil. Finally, the chaplain came
by and sat down beside me. He spoke in general terms
about birth and so on. I commented that no one had
spoken to me about my baby or taken me to see him.

Eventually, I was allowed to see my new son,
who was on a ventilator, struggling for his life. He had
been born with "main line" defects, the most visible
being a cleft, or split, upper lip and pallet, exposing the
fleshy interior of his mouth and creating a very deformed
appearance. However, the more severe problems were
unseen: a defective heart and deformities to his
digestive organs.

Soon, nurses rolled Cheryl in on a gurney to be
placed near our son, seeing him for the first time. She
was appalled and devastated.

That same day, our new baby, Joshua, and I flew
by helicopter to a more specialized and larger hospital in
Virginia. Several doctors evaluated and examined
Joshua. All of them shared the opinion that he would not
live more than two weeks. They conducted various tests
and drew more blood samples than I could count. They
told me Joshua had Trisomy 13, a fatal condition for
which there was no cure or treatment. They then
recommended he not be nourished in order to prevent

prolonging his life. Of course, I refused this advice. Later, medical tests results came in which showed their preliminary diagnosis to be erroneous.

Before the tests results were received, however, the doctors relayed their opinion to a physician at our home base in North Carolina. This physician entered Cheryl's hospital room and informed her that her baby was going to die. She then exited the room, leaving my wife alone, without family, friends, or pastoral support.

In a few days, Cheryl was also flown to Virginia to be with Joshua. She was exhausted emotionally and sore from the emergency surgical delivery. Additionally, her movement was severely restricted by the stitches. Furthermore, her milk had come in fully, but Joshua could not nurse due to his cleft lip and pallet. Cheryl's condition was extremely painful. One day she prayed for relief from the aching and the very next morning she awakened to find herself back to normal. Cheryl called it "my little miracle."

In the intensive care unit, we trooped along daily with Joshua. Our bonding as father and son became stronger every day. Although Cheryl carried Joshua for nine months, I quickly caught up in affection and attachment to this little warrior. Joshua knew the

difference between an attendant holding him and my
holding him. In my arms, he would calm down to a
restful peace, even though there were many wires and
tubes interfered with his physical comfort. He was a
wonderful son and we both had an understanding of our
time together. I baptized him in his crib with a single
drop of water.

Meanwhile, back at our base, a tremendous
amount of prayer went up for Joshua. My faith and
testimony were unshaken. I prayed constantly and
believed Joshua would survive.

However, one night after surgery, Joshua's
bodily systems "crashed" and his strength sunk to such a
level the doctors said he should have died. The next day,
we were able to hold him once more. Joshua died after
ten days as a result of septic shock. He had been born
with a heart condition that his physicians predicted
would take his life. And although he had been born with
this physical weakness, he never lost heart.

We brought Joshua's body back to North
Carolina. Family and a good group of solid friends from
work and church attended his memorial and funeral
services. I was awfully young and inexperienced in such
a strange setting. But I think you have to be young to

survive an ordeal like we experienced.

Struggles of life and death, especially trials in the life of infants, give men pause to consider many questions, some which they voice and some, which remain unspoken.

The first is "Why?"

The answer in Joshua's case has nothing to do with right or wrong, morality or immorality. Joshua was born with physical problems that simply occur in a certain number of children, whether they are from Christian homes or not. A certain percentage of babies are born like Joshua, a certain number crippled, a certain number deaf. These facts exist regardless of their parents, morality, or excellence of prenatal care. It has nothing to do with the righteous or the unrighteous. It is just a fact in this fallen world. Nature contains realities unrelated to our conduct.

There is another question of whether a life so short counts. What is in a life of ten days? Joshua's life started a chain of events that touched a military community of over 50,000 people. It unified the believers in love and concern, generating countless hours of fervent prayer and wrestling with God. I am sure that it also prompted many a parent to thank God for their healthy children.

Joshua's life and the Christian love that surrounded it also arrested the attention of unbelievers. Specifically, some of the medical staff observed a difference in the kind of people concerned about Joshua. I saw one of the doctors in church following Joshua's death. Many who were peripherally involved with me reached out in concern. All observed supernatural oversight of our plight. In the military, a commander cannot soften hearts like that. A subordinate cannot touch a soul this way. But, somehow a little baby can. Without authority or might, Joshua reached the distant and the insulated in a very human way.

There is also testimony – magnified for all to see. The world sees the love displayed by Christians toward one another and they know that there are Christians among them, living out the same problems and working through the same obstacles they face.

Furthermore, there is also the unspoken testimony of a life sustained by Christ. When death comes to a loved one, it can crush a man, defeat him, and leave him in despair. But when death comes to a Christian, he has hope. I was cheered so much by the account in 1 Samuel about the death of David's baby boy. David, whose son was ill, refused food while he wept for his suffering son. Yet, in God's providence, his son died. To the amazement of his royal courtiers, David took heart, rose and began to eat again. He answered his astonished attendants, "I shall go to him, but he shall not return to me." (1 Samuel 12:23) From this we know that God takes little babies to His heavenly home to care for them and that we will see them there.

So, I was and am comforted by knowing God has welcomed Joshua to heaven, health, and joy. When Joshua's life on earth ended, it began again in heaven and this is one more reason I look forward to eternity. We will have a family reunion one bright day. Knowing this will make it easier to leave this earth.

Another question is very near to the lips of everyone concerned about you: "How are you doing?" My answer to any inquiry about my emotional well-being is that I have not gotten over it, but I have gotten beyond it. Even though it has been 23 years ago, I still cry when I recall the details of the helpless baby I held, not expecting him to die.

Yet, there are good reasons for my son's passing through this world so quickly and on to heaven. I don't understand the reasons fully, but I know God is good and that God was good to Joshua and me every day we had together. Truthfully, Joshua never really belonged to me. God simply loaned him to me for a short time. And why would God give up ten days with Joshua to let me have him? I know I did not deserve a precious boy like him, yet God gave him to me. That must be love. He must be Love.

I Surely Miss You
By Curtis Mosley

Joshua, your entrance here was fast and furious.
Racing nurses, frantic doctors amidst the fuss,

Ushered from delivery to tests and surgery,
With wires and tubes, never quite free.

Your hospital room was ever so sterile.
The familiar smell of closeness to peril.

Your attendants were unruffled in their reports.
Yet, I hung on every word of their retorts.

Maintaining the coolness of their calling,
While I completely in love with you was falling.

Though your life was short, with barely a start,
Your message has endured, and captured my heart.

Though the dreams I had held seemed so altered.
I prayed with a faith that never faltered.

Trusting Him In Your Grief/Charlotte Holt

I called out each day and into the night.
You fought on with all your might.

A great many your testimony heard.
Even though you could not utter a word.

From your little bed in the hospital room,
You opened the Church to her full bloom.

So many prayers and deeds of kindness
The saints were moved your life to caress.

And others, who observed this great goodness,
Were touched in a way that only a baby could bless.

You fulfilled your purpose and made your mark
Through distress and pain in that room so stark.

You have a heart and soul and irresistible charms,
Becoming quiet and calm when in my arms.

The special relation between father and son,
Your place in my heart was easily won.

I'll come to you one day 'tis true,
But Joshua, for now, I surely miss you!

Curtis and Cheryl reside in Kingwood, Texas, a suburb of Houston. They have one son in his twenties, who attends college at Sam Houston State University in Huntsville. Curtis is an employee benefits broker and Cheryl is a flight attendant. Both are members of First Assembly of God church in Humble. They have been married 25+ years. Curtis is also the author of two books, Rain Catcher and Team Weaver.

Charlotte's Comments

What an awesome God we serve. What faith these parents experienced. Curt saw God's handiwork even in the midst of the storm. He recognized how God used his circumstances, pain and suffering to help others see the reality of faith in action. He acknowledged the testimony his son brought to the hearts of others. These parents didn't grieve or feel any less deeply than the rest of us, yet they were able to recognize God's sovereignty and goodness in the midst of it all. May we do the same.

Prayer: *Lord, help us to recognize and acknowledge Your goodness and sovereignty in the good and bad times. Help us to see Your hand at work in our times of trials. Help us to keep our eyes focused on You at all times. In Jesus Name. Amen.*

Chapter Eight
The Promised Land
By Lisa Gatlin

"Joshua and Caleb come sit down," said a mother in the pew in front of us.

My wide-eyed four-year old Jonathan climbed up in my lap. "Are they my brothers?" he whispered.

Tears stung my eyes as I shook my head. I need your strength God, my heart cried out.

After church I explained to him that his brothers waited for us in heaven. These boys only shared their name and age.

My first born, Joshua came eight weeks prematurely. He did fine until day three when he began to have seizures. The doctors told us his brain swelled and they didn't know why. They began running tests but could not find a cause. Soon Joshua fell into in a comatose state. I sat by his bed daily, praying.

My husband and I led Children's Church. Everyone in our church family prayed and offered their support. I kept waiting for a miracle. Day after day I watched my son grow worse and yet, I stood on faith. I just knew God would do something miraculous and astound the doctors. However, one month and seventeen days later Joshua entered Heaven.

At the funeral home I opened the Bible they gave me. It opened to Joshua 1:9: *Be strong and of good courage; be not afraid, neither be thou dismayed: for the Lord thy God is with thee whithersoever thou goest.* God began to heal my heart and soothe my soul.

A few months later I found out I was pregnant again. I was so excited that soon I would have a baby to fill my empty arms. Only he came too soon. Caleb arrived five weeks early. He seemed so strong and healthy. I hated leaving him at the hospital. It didn't seem fair that once again I would go home empty-handed.

After a few weeks they allowed us to take him home. What joy I felt to walk through my front door carrying my son. I could not get enough of just gazing at this beautiful child.

Then one day while he slept, he began to turn blue. I grabbed him up, thinking he was choking since I had just fed him. He turned pink again. Shaken, I laid him next to me and sat watching him sleep. Once again he began to turn blue. I grabbed him and called the doctor. She said to bring him right in. Upon examining him, she found nothing wrong but sent us straight to the hospital.

The doctors hooked Caleb up to monitors for twenty-four hours. They informed us he had sleep apnea, better known as crib death. They assured us it was fairly common in premature babies and that he would probably outgrow it by the time he reached a year old. They sent him home with a monitor attached to alert us if he stopped breathing while he slept. Before leaving the hospital I trained in infant CPR. I prayed I would never have to use it.

The next morning I woke up to see my husband staring in the crib. The look on his face told me something was wrong.

"I think he's having seizures," he said quietly. Since I had not seen Joshua's seizures before he became comatose, I did not know how subtle they could be. Caleb's little arm would suddenly jerk a few times and then relax. Surely this couldn't be a seizure.

But the anguished look on my husband's face made me fearful. We brought him straight to the hospital where they began test of all kinds. They even ran tests on my husband and me. They had no answers for me. His brain was swelling and he was indeed having seizures. At this point, he began to do exactly as Joshua had done. The doctors said it must be genetic, their only conclusion.

Along with the monitor, they sent us home with medications to stop Caleb's seizures. There was nothing more they could do for him. They said he could live for months or years, but he would surely die.

Day and night his monitor would go off. I would touch or gently shake him and he would breathe again. Caleb began to grow stiff. The doctors explained that as areas of the brain died he lost muscle control. They said it was actually rigor mortis setting in. I trained in physical therapy to move his muscles for him.

What pierced my heart the most though were Caleb's eyes. When he did open them, they were dull and empty.

The Bible warns us to not get weary in well doing, but I did. I grew so tired of the constant care and concerns. I needed to get away and yet I was afraid to leave him. I couldn't go to the store or even church. Few people, including my husband, relieved me for fear of Caleb dying while in their care. I began to cry out to God to either heal him or take him, for I could not go on like this.

One Sunday morning my mother showed up and told me to go to church and then get away to myself for a while. We had an evangelist visiting our church that morning. No one knew I was coming. When he walked out on the platform, he looked straight at me and told me to come forward. God had a word for me.

"My child you are tired. The battle is over. Rest in me," he said. As the evangelist prayed for me, it felt like warm oil poured over my head and the tiredness drained out of my feet.

That night I fell into a deep sleep. I am usually a very light sleeper. I became aware of Caleb's monitor going off but it was like I was traveling through a long tunnel to get to it. Finally, sat up and looked over into his bassinet. He was blue and not breathing. I grabbed him and began CPR while my husband called the hospital. They did not have an ambulance available so my husband drove while I continued CPR.

When we arrived at the local hospital, they grabbed him from me and began working on him. As I stood just a few feet away, my heart cried out to God, Please don't take him I'm not ready.

I watched them inject a needle directly into his heart. It started beating. When stabilized, they sent him by ambulance to the hospital where he was born.

There they informed us, Caleb had a heartbeat but no brain activity. Days passed slowly as the doctors gave us time to adjust. They gently encouraged us to face the fact he could live on life support for months or years but he would never recover. A decision needed to be made. Once again I fell on my knees. I cried out in anguish from the depth of my soul, "Why God? Why me? Why again?" I felt His warmth surround me, and peace flooded my soul.

We told the doctors they could disconnect him on Friday. I began to pray. "Please, Lord, don't let this decision be mine. You gave him life. You take it away. I'm ready now."

Thursday night the hospital called to tell us Caleb had died. As I cried my grief out, I thanked God for answering my prayers.

Months later I discovered I was pregnant again. My doctor said, "I do not perform abortions but in your case I recommend one due to medical reasons." He was concerned I could not physically or emotionally go through another pregnancy so soon since it had been determined the problem was genetic and this baby could die as well.

I considered his suggestion for one brief moment. In the natural sense, I did not want to the heartache again, but in the spirit I wanted to follow God.

With my decision made, I voiced my promise to the Lord. "God, if You take a hundred babies from me I will not abort one of them." He was the giver of life and He had placed this child in me. I placed this child in God's hands.

Jonathan's name means God's gift. He is indeed a precious gift. Two years after he was born, God blessed me with a beautiful daughter named Jessica. I don't know why He allowed me to keep two and why He kept two but I do know this, my God's grace is sufficient for me.

God filled my heart and life with two wonderful stepchildren, Dusten and Koryssa. I thank Him for allowing me the honor of raising four children. I also thank Him for the sweet assurance that not only will I enter the promised land of heaven but also I have two sweet sons, Joshua and Caleb, who went in first and are waiting for me.

Miracles
By Lisa Gatlin

Miracles, big and small, make life so sweet. They are the essence of faith. I have been blessed to have witnessed and experienced countless miracles in my life. The sweetest one I hold next to my heart occurred the day I buried Joshua, my son.

Dark angry clouds gathered all morning. Deep rumbling thunder vibrated all it touched. Sitting in the middle of my bed pouring my pain and distress out to God, I prayed a simple prayer. "Lord, funerals are depressing enough. Please don't let it rain."

It rained on the way to the funeral parlor. It rained on the way to the gravesite. Looking up to heaven with tears streaming down my face, I reminded Him, "Please, Lord."

As family and friends walked slowly toward the tombs, huddled under their umbrellas, a sweet miracle began. With each step the rains softened. Directly above Joshua's tomb the clouds were rolled back in an enormous circle. People began to search pockets and purses, I thought, for handkerchiefs. A smile tugged on the corner of my mouth as each one began to produce sunglasses. Penetrating through that circle of dark clouds blasted a beam of sunlight so bright we could not look upon the white glare of his

Tombstone.

After the service ended we turned and began slowly walking away. I glanced over my shoulder and watched the beam of sunlight fade as the clouds closed with each step we took. By the time we climbed into our cars, the rain had begun again. I looked up to heaven and with a grateful heart I said, "Thank-you, Lord." I was reminded once more that miracles, both big and small, are what make life so sweet.

The Changing Table
By Lisa Gatlin

Joshua, my first born, my son, I miss you and often wonder what you would be like. You would be thirteen years old with dark hair and big brown eyes - probably very spunky. You fought hard to live for a month and a half. I wish you could have come home with me. We covered your room in yellow gingham and your grandfather made you a beautiful changing table. I still have it today . . .

Caleb, my second born, my son, I miss you too and often wonder what you would be like. You would be twelve years old with dark curly hair and big brown eyes - probably very sweet and charming. You captivated everyone with your sweetness for three months. Though I kept you at my side, your room too was yellow gingham. You lay on the beautiful changing table your grandfather made. I still have it today . . .

Jonathan, my third born, my son, I know you and often wonder what you will become. You're only eleven years old right now with your dark hair and big brown eyes. You bring such comfort with your gentle, caring nature. Your room went from yellow gingham to the Dallas Cowboys. The changing table your grandfather made held first you, and then later your trucks and GI Joes. I still have it today . . .

Jessica, my baby, my daughter, I know you and often wonder what you will become. You're only eight years old right now with dark hair and big brown eyes. You bring such joy with your love of life and your carefree spirit. Your room went from pink softness to Precious Moments and ballerinas. The changing table your grandfather made held first you and then your baby dolls. I still have it today.

Joshua, your grandfather made you a beautiful changing table . . .. I still have it today.

Lisa Gatlin was born in Boynton Beach, Florida but moved to Southeast Louisiana at an early age. She earned her Bachelor's Degree from Southeastern University in Hammond, Louisiana in Elementary Education. Her love for teaching had her teaching her dolls and cats at the age of four. She presently resides in Huffman, Texas. Lisa has served as a youth pastor and children's church pastor. She has taught second grade for twenty years. Lisa is the mother of four and grandmother of five.

Charlotte's Comments

This mother went through pain unending for a long time and lost two children, one after the other. I venture to say she grew stronger because of her experiences. She indicates an appreciation she wouldn't otherwise have for the children God left with her and the stepchildren He brought into her life.

Even when we lose our precious children, we can keep their memories alive. Her example of the changing table gives us an idea of things we remember and treasure. We can experience God's hand as He guides us through difficult times. He gives us miracles in the midst of our pain, like he did for Lisa with the sunshine at the funeral.

Often, He sends us other priceless gifts, people, or things to help relieve the pain of our loss. Even though, our children can't be replaced, He gives us special gifts to treasure, whether other children, stepchildren, or things. God takes good care of His children. He wants only good things for us in our lives — the same way we do for our own.

I pray we will be able to release our child to God with open outstretched hands, so He might fill them to overflowing with what He has for us. We may never know why we couldn't keep our child. We know only in part but God sees the entire picture. We can trust Him to take care of us and give us His very best even if it isn't what we planned.

Trusting Him In Your Grief/Charlotte Holt

Prayer: *Thank You, Lord, for the priceless gifts You give to us. Thank You, for the time with our children. Thank You for the special gifts and treasures You afford us. Help us to release our children to Your care. Thank You for the overflow You give to us. We pray we will someday understand the reason we couldn't keep our children longer. Help us to trust You because You know the whole picture. In Jesus Name. Amen.*

Chapter Nine
Where Is God When You've Lost Your Child?
By Monica Cane

It was supposed to be another day of adventures for my baby Kevin and me. He was over three months old, and a whopping twelve pounds. His eyes were the brightest of blue. His blonde hair resembled a thin layer of peach fuzz and his double, or perhaps triple, chin had so many rolls, it could hold more lint than a Kenmore dryer. Kevin did all the adorable things baby boys did at his age. He laughed, he rolled, he smiled, and on that day it should not have been any different—but it was.

I awakened from a much-needed nap and was preparing to spend the day teaching my son valuable lessons. Like why strained peas are actually good for you. And how cows make milk and so do mommies. Clearly, I had high expectations of his comprehension level as I considered how we would spend our day.

I strolled unsuspectingly into his room, assuming I would find my sweet, lively bundle of joy stirring from his own nap. What I found was entirely different. What I found changed my life forever. Without reason, explanation, or justification, my vivacious bundle of joy died in his sleep. Sudden Infant Death Syndrome took Kevin away in the blink of an eye.

My first reaction was to scream out at the top of my lungs to a God I didn't really know. A God I only heard about. A God I thought lived somewhere up in the sky but nowhere near me. And so I screamed. I shouted. I demanded this God return my son and when He didn't, the world, as I knew it, the one filled with baby coos, giggles and kisses, shifted into a lonely dark abyss. All I wanted to know but was too afraid to ask was, where is God?

It would be quite some time before I discovered the answer to my question. Though many tragedies are suffered throughout the world, losing a child somehow seems to be the greatest offense. It makes no sense because of their age and their innocence. Where is God? This is the question on the tip of the tongue for most of those affected by it.

As with the majority of parents who have lost a child, the grieving process was far from instantaneous. It took many years to work through, many years of wondering about God. It was during a portion of this time that I discovered a powerful source of healing—

The Bible. Within its pages, I soon discovered the presence of God.

Much like the Israelites of Exodus, Gods Word became a pillar of strength to guide me. *Neither the pillar of cloud by day or the pillar of fire by night left its place in front of the people.* Exodus 13:22 (NIV)

The Israelites found themselves traveling through the desert, a hot and barren land, in order to reach their destination with freedom. The desert was not the route they would have chosen, much like losing Kevin was not what I would have chosen for myself. Nonetheless it was the path laid before them. God proved faithful to meet them in the midst of their desert journey. He reassured them of His presence, though the journey was long and hard. He did the same for me.

My years of grieving left me feeling as though I wandered through a desert. I had lost my child and every step of my journey toward healing was long and hard. However, my questions - Where is God and where is He when my son died? My answers were revealed as I stumbled across Scripture after Scripture testifying of His presence in all situations. Even if I thought life had treated me unfairly, I could not deny the evidence revealed in the Bible. This prompted me to make a choice to believe in God's presence in my life, both then and now.

Realizing God had been there all along did not give me an answer as to why Kevin died. It did not explain why I, being a good mommy, lost my baby; while other mothers bent towards neglect, were allowed to keep theirs. No. Choosing to believe that God is omnipresent did not bring answers to those specific questions. However, 1 Corinthians 13:12 did shed a great deal of light. *Now I know in part: then I shall know fully, even as I am fully known.* Corinthians 13:12 (NIV)

I didn't have all the answers but understanding God never left His place in front of me, gave me the reassurance that He would carry me through what I didn't understand. And then one day He would explain it all.

Our life's journey will bring us both good and bad. Some experiences will have explanations, others will not. Choosing what you believe will make the difference as to how your journey proceeds. Where is God when you've lost your child? Where is God when you hurt? Where is God when life makes no sense and you need help? He is already with you. He is standing by, longing to be your pillar of cloud by day and your pillar of fire by night. You only need to believe.

Monica Cane, author and speaker, has touched the hearts and lives of readers everywhere. As the founder of A Breath of Inspiration Ministry, a freelance writing ministry geared toward strengthening the day-to-day lives of believers, Monica uses her gift of encouragement to create inspirational books and articles, appearing nationwide. Monica's simplistic style draws readers to a more intimate level of fellowship with God by allowing them to laugh, cry and relate to the truth of God's presence in their "ordinary" and "not-so-ordinary" lives. Monica along with her husband and three children, reside in Northern California.
(www.abreathofinspiration.com)

Charlotte's Comments

According to Marc Petezell, chairman of the American SIDS Institute, the death rate for SIDS since 1983 has fallen fifty percent. However, 2,500 babies in the United States are lost each year by the disease and thousands more throughout the world.

There seems to be a great support system via the Internet for parents who have lost a child to SIDS. However, the best support system I know is the one Monica found in the Holy Scripture as she searched for answers to the age-old question of "God Where Are

You?'"

Many ask this same question in whatever difficult trial they may encounter. If any of us find ourselves asking this question, we can take a look where Monica did and find the answer for ourselves. We will find Him there in the midst of our storm or in the pages of His book.

Prayer: *Thank You, Lord, that we can find the answers to all of life's problems in Your book. Help us to search and know Your Word. Help us to study to show ourselves approved unto You. Help us to find those answers You provide through Your Word. Thank You for the support offered to those who lose a child through SIDS. May the numbers of deaths continue to decrease. Thank You, Lord, that You are always there – even when we don't feel Your presence. Help us to know and understand we are the one who moves. In Jesus Name. Amen.*

Chapter Ten
Seth Michael Ludwig
By Lisa Ludwig

I like to say his name every now and then. It reminds me that he was real—that for three months, and nineteen days, he was a part of my life. Seffy, as my husband and I liked to call him, was born on December 15, 1990. A little more than eight pounds, he was a healthy baby, with a big brown eyes and a ready smile. We couldn't help but laugh when we saw him. Had Seth lived, his nickname would have been "Ski," due to the size of his feet.

Seth was a quiet baby. I believe he was a thinker; maybe the curious sort, like me. His eyes followed me everywhere, and oftentimes, his brow would furrow as though he were pondering some new detail of his world. We spent that winter enjoying all of the "firsts" with him. First Christmas. First taste of baby cereal. First...Spring.

April 3, 1991. I awoke late that morning, and remember thinking how glad I was that the children, Seth and my older son Ben, had overslept and allowed me some much needed rest. I bathed and dressed, reveling in the opportunity to actually be alone in the bathroom. I took my time, confident that should the children wake, my husband, who worked nights, would see to their needs. To my surprise, no television blared from the living room after I finished. I think I expected Ben, who normally rose very early, to have gotten up and roused the rest of the house, as was his duty, or so he thought.

My mom stopped by while I was making breakfast. I distinctly remember her asking me if she could wake the boys. I smiled, and pleaded with her not to, since we'd had a late night the day before. Like a good grandma, she left some things for the kids and went on to town. How I wished later that I'd asked her to stay. Still, a part of me has always been glad that I found Seth in his crib, and not her.

By mid-morning, I decided that enough was enough, and went upstairs to wake the boys. Seth's room was still dark with the curtains pulled. Even in April, Michigan is slow to stir from a cozy slumber, especially with the wind beating at the windows.

The details of Seth's death are foggy to me. Perhaps as some sort of defense mechanism, my mind has blocked out the more painful memories. I remember calling his name, in a quiet tone of voice so as not to startle him. At last, I put my hand to his back. That was the first moment that I knew something was dreadfully wrong.

My husband and I called the paramedics. Of course, it was much too late. Seth died sometime during the night. We called my parents, my husband's parents. They must have broken every speed limit coming to my house from work. It did not take long for them to arrive. Someone else made the calls after that. I never found out who.

The next three days passed in a blur. I still count that as an example of God's absolute mercy. I don't know how we could have made it through the week otherwise. There are flashes of grace that I remember, like the police officer, whose voice conveyed such kindness as he told us the exact cause of Seth's death, and the woman from church, who came to our house and began making sandwiches for our family without a word to anyone. These examples of Christ-like service have stuck with me, embedded so firmly in my memory that even if time should erase their names, these people would hold a special place in my heart.

Above all, I remember God's presence, and the

comfort I found in small book entitled, "Death of a Little Child," by J. Vernon McGee. Tattered and worn, the book came to me from a stranger. I clung to that book, even added a few tearstains to the pages already discolored by telltale watermarks. Several years ago, I passed it on; to another mother I'm saddened to say. I wrote a few words inside. I pray that it was a message of hope to this woman I did not know, and perhaps others, should she someday decide to do the same and pass the book on.

Though I couldn't admit it then, one sentence has impressed me through the years, eleven words so eloquently spoken that I find myself repeating them again and again in cemeteries and funeral homes, and two years ago, in my mother-in-law's room when she died in her bed from cancer.

"The presence of death does not mean the absence of God."

I have learned that in fact, the opposite is true. It is in those times when I have stood in the presence of death that God has been most real, most tangible, and at His absolute most astonishing and awesome. His love enveloped me, sustained me, and when I look back upon that year of my life, I know it was then that I truly gave my heart to Him. Grief is a gift, for only when we are broken can God begin to heal.

Surely, this has been God's lesson to me throughout my life. There is hope in death. God is not absent. His desire is for us to pour our hope and faith in Him, and for the blood of His Son to redeem us and grant us everlasting life.

I'm looking forward to a reunion with Seffy in heaven someday. I'll know him by his smile, I think, and by the way his eyes follow me as I see my Lord and Savior face to face for the first time.

What a wonderful party the Father has planned. By God's grace, the invitation to attend has been extended to all.

Pass it on.

Elizabeth Ludwig is an award winning author and accomplished speaker and teacher. She often attends conferences and seminars, where she lectures on editing for fiction writers, crafting effective novel proposals, and conducting successful editor/agent interviews. She is the owner and editor of the popular literary blog, The Borrowed Book. Visit her at www.elizabethludwig.com

Charlotte's Comments

Yes, God's grace is extended to those of us who experience this process of loss through death. When we go through the fog of the days of pain and anguish, He is there beside us. "The presence of death does not mean the absence of God." I find it quite the contrary.

When we travel through the stages of grief, He comforts us, giving us the grace and mercy we need. Whether we feel foggy, blurry, peaceful, numb, angry, sad and teary, or absolutely nothing, He walks with us in each condition. His grace remains sufficient for each emotion and painful experience. During the worst of times, He wraps us in a bubble, insulated dwelling, or as if kept in the eye of a terrible storm or tornado. He gives us peace in the midst of our disaster.

During these times, God proves definitely the most awesome. He shows up in strength and power when we find ourselves at our weakest. The loss of a child proves to be the weakest of moments, but God appears in His mighty power and strength if we lean on Him.

Prayer: *Dear Lord, thank You that we can lean on You in our weakness. Thank You for being there any day or hour. Thank You that You neither slumber nor sleep, but You watch over us continually. Thank You for the comfort we feel and can pass on to others. Help us to comfort as You have comforted us. Hold us through every storm of life. In Jesus Name. Amen.*

Chapter Eleven
I Choose New Life
Author's Name Withheld

I lay claim to six children, all girls, when in reality he has three, I have one and together we have three. For those of you who are quick at math that equals seven, but not all are girls. In 1994 my world turned on end when our two and a half year old little boy Gabe died.

At that time in my life, I had separated from my first husband of three years. I lived with my high school sweetheart and we settled into the daily grind of a blended family, splitting the children's time with both of our ex spouses. When my kids returned to me one afternoon, my usually bright, happy, baby boy was withdrawn, whiney and just not himself. It's the change of family structure, I thought, a flu bug or something, which would rectify itself in a matter of days.

Throughout the weekend Gabe did little things to make me wonder but nothing I worried about. After all, as his mom I would know if I needed to ask for help. Monday morning I went to work and left my children home with John, my husband by now, and John's three girls.

"You're needed at home," my boss informed me shortly after lunch.

My boss did not tell me the circumstances as we rode to meet John's father. I casually strolled to the truck. The look on my father-in-law's face told me something was terribly wrong, something other than the typical chaos of summer.

"There has been as accident and Gabe is hurt," Dad said.

Still being in mom mode, I thought, *okay, a broken arm, broken leg, but nothing I can't handle.*

After an hour of driving through road construction, we finally arrived to find chaos at our house. I jumped out of the truck before it stopped and ran into the house to find Gabe absent. They told me he had been airlifted to the hospital and wasn't responsive. I had just missed him.

It took us three hours to get to the hospital. When we arrived, I found my baby boy on life support. For the next twenty-four hours, I found myself faced with decisions of organ donation and test after test for my son. I tried to convince myself there was a God and he couldn't possibly take my baby. Gabe belonged to me and I wasn't ready to let him go.

The afternoon of July 19, I held the sweetest little boy that ever walked through my life as his heart stopped beating. I laid him on the bed, told him how very much I loved him and kissed him one last time. I looked at him and he looked like my sleeping baby. The sun shone through the window on him and I felt God saying to me, "He's safe with me now and how precious he is."

I thought that was the worst day of my life. I had no idea there would be more.

The funeral came and went. The service was beautiful from what I remember. The next couple of days I stayed in a fog.

Then the authorities charged John with Gabe's death. The doctor said Gabe had shaken baby's syndrome. They accused John of shaking him to death. They charged me with knowing of the abuse and said I let it happen.

Wow, I allowed it to happen? How absurd. Let me say my husband is one of the best father's I know, a little lenient at times, but there are no words to describe what his children mean to him.

In the end, they found Gabe wasn't shaken to

death but something happened and someone had to pay. My husband was convicted of felony injury to a child because something happened to Gabe while in his care. John was sentenced to prison for two to ten years.

He went on his 'vacation' as we referred to it in the fall of 1996. He came back home to us in the fall of 1998 after serving the minimum of two years. They never restricted him from any of his children, even though when he began his vacation we had three-month-old Amy, which through all of our trials could only have been a God thing.

During John's 'vacation,' I met a woman, now one of my good friends, who looked at me as nothing short of a challenge I'm sure. I went to her house to meet her as a potential sitter for Amy. I sat on her couch, sizing her up from top to bottom. "I know you're a religious person but don't push it on me or my child and we will do just fine." So, take that, I thought.

About six months later, she convinced me to try an Experiencing God Bible study. During the study I accepted Christ but I still had what seemed like a lifetime of baggage to unpack. She and I look back on our first meeting and laugh. In essence, I was telling God He couldn't make me do it. I was mistaken.

When John came home, I started to feel the loss of Gabe. For the previous three and a half years, I took care of other people so I couldn't focus on myself. I don't know if I *could* focus on myself at that time. I barely forced myself not to act on the million and one ways I thought of to stop all my pain and be with my little boy. For the next three years, or so, I dealt in bits and pieces. I struggled with depression, anger, bitterness, resentment...the list goes on and on. I remained angry at God. How could He take so much from me? After all, Gabe was mine, or so, I thought. *We can gather our thoughts, but the Lord gives the right answer.* Proverbs 16:1 (NLT)

Eventually John and I began attending church. I'm not sure why he started going, but I went to make friends. I found out in short order - I had to be a friend to make one. I wasn't ready to do that. *People may be pure in their own eyes, but the Lord examines their motives.* Proverbs 16:2 (NLT)

Still in the anger mode, I wanted my questions answered. One Sunday, someone cornered me and told me I needed a recovery class. I thought, okay, now, THIS is the place to find friends. I had no clue there were other people in the world with problems like mine.

I figured we'd just get together and hang for a few hours once a week. God really worked on me in that class. Six months of recovery and years later, I have more friends than I ever dreamed.

Commit your work to the Lord, and then your plans will succeed. Proverbs 16:3 (NLT)

I'm on the backside of that whole other life and I have found my life is full of choices. My choices are to be thankful for everything God has given me no matter how trivial it seems. I could lay on the couch with my bag of Hershey kisses and a Jerry Springer marathon (because someone's life is always worse than mine) and take myself to that "poor me" place and stay there for days.

I choose every day to be thankful for my husband and our girls. I am most thankful for the two and a half years we had with Gabe and the God he is with.

There are times I still wonder why he had to leave us. I sometimes have moments, hours and days full of "what ifs" and "if onlys" but I know God had a purpose for Gabe. Now instead of mommy and daddy being his buddy, as we used to be, he has Jesus, a buddy that will never let him hurt again.

On a radio program I heard Chuck Swindoll quote Dr. Redpath: "The conversion of a soul is the miracle of a moment, the manufacture of a saint is the task of a lifetime." A person can become a child of God. Then God begins a process of manufacturing into that person the qualities of sainthood. Christian people are not immune to hard times. Hard times are like the anvil on which our Lord shapes us into the likeness of His Son.

Some of you are on that anvil. The furnace is heated and you don't know what shape is going to be taken. As a result of the furnace, I can assure you those difficult times will be the making of greatness.

We endure thorns, furnaces and filings in order to become mature. We are all growing older but we are not all growing up. Unless we submit to the blows, buffetings and the pain God allows, we are not becoming all He intends us to be.

Faith is seeing the invisible, knowing the unknowable, believing the unbelievable, so you might achieve the impossible.

I have a faith now like never before. I believe Gabe is walking with Jesus. I know there was a purpose in all of this. I feel confident that no matter how bad my days get or how unmanageable I think they are, God sees me and won't give me anything He and I can't handle together. To be here today with this joy I have for the life I am given, I have achieved the impossible.

For I can do everything with the help of Christ who gives me the strength I need. Philippians 4:13 (NLT)

Charlotte's Comments

Names of the people involved in the above story were changed and the author's name withheld in order to protect the innocent, but according to the author the story is true. God's grace covers us at all times. He continues to work good things out of bad situations. He changes lives. We can do all things through Christ. So, we must trust Him in any and all situations, especially in our grief. This mother had reasons to grieve, instead she chose to turn to God and let Him bring her through a terrible time and loss in her life.

Because of her faith and trust in Him she found herself able to achieve victory. She realized the power of the strength Christ gave her. She may have started out seeking for friends but she found the best friend ever, the friend that sticks closer than a brother. He never leaves us or forsakes us.

Knowing Him as her friend, she trusted her

precious baby, Gabe, to His care and keeping. She found peace and comfort in knowing Gabe resides with her best friend. We have no problem leaving our children with our best friends here on earth. What a comfort to know our children live now and forever with a friend like no other, one that laid down His life for them and us.

Prayer: *Thank You, Lord for being that friend who sticks closer than a brother. We depend on Your strength, mercy, grace and friendship. Help us to know You better than any other friend. Help us to rely on You in every area of our life. We thank You that we will see our children again. Thank You for keeping them safe. Thank You for the peace it brings to us knowing they are there with You. In Jesus Name. Amen.*

Chapter Twelve
Where Have You Gone, Billy-Boy?
As told to Janice Thompson
By Shirley Moseley

I married young. That's how we did it back in the 50's. A woman dreamed of being a wife and mother. Nothing could surpass that joy. I was well on my way when I married my high school sweetheart, Billy, and we began a life together. He dreamed of big, exciting things. I dreamed of a simple life, filled with children and a happy home.

Billy and I moved to Texas – far away from our home in Illinois. We found ourselves in an adventurous new place, full of life and even fuller of possibilities. He had an entrepreneurial spirit and wanted to start his own business. I had a mother's heart and awaited our first-born.

Billy, Jr. was born in December of 1956. He was my first-born and his father's namesake. He was a beautiful child with a contagious smile – and he was exactly what we'd hoped and prayed he would be: healthy, strong, perfect. I thanked the Lord for such a marvelous blessing.

A couple of years later, our first daughter was born. We named her Janice. Just a few short months later, we discovered we were expecting again. This time things were different. I already had my hands full with two little ones. Why was the Lord giving me a third – and so soon? I don't want to say this one was unwanted... just unexpected.

Our second daughter, Connie, was born on April 7, 1960. While I was in the hospital with her (and they kept you nearly a week back in those days) our other two children became very ill. They both had German measles. On top of that, they developed upper respiratory symptoms. Billy, in particular, was so sick that my husband took him to the doctor before I ever arrived home.

"It's just German measles," the doctor said. "It's good to expose kids to the measles. All kids should be exposed."

When you're young – and sometimes even when you're old – you listen to doctors and automatically assume they know what they're talking about. In this case, we were sadly mistaken. For reasons we still don't fully understand, this doctor didn't give our son the care he needed.

I arrived home from the hospital and knew that something was terribly wrong. Billy was so very sick. Though I was only just out of the hospital a short time, I called on my mother, who picked me up and drove us to the doctor's office. This time, Billy was diagnosed with pneumonia. However, due to a lack of beds in the contagion ward of the hospital nearest our home, he was sent home.

By the next day, I knew we were in trouble. Billy was much worse. We took him to another doctor, who immediately hospitalized him in a different location. He had developed double pneumonia. The doctors there did everything they could. Billy was given large doses of antibiotics and received the best care, but it just wasn't enough.

We watched in shock and despair as our little boy slowly slipped away from us. The day after he was admitted to the hospital, Billy lost his fight with the pneumonia. He went to be with Jesus at the tender age of four.

It's so hard to share what happened after that. I had to bury my firstborn – the child I had longed for and loved for four wonderful years. I had to somehow pull things together enough to care for a fifteen-month-old (who was still very ill) and a newborn I hadn't expected.

I didn't feel like doing any of those things. I just wanted my sweet baby boy back. I wanted Billy. I didn't care about much else.

To be honest, I struggled with how I felt about our tiny newborn, Connie. I loved her, certainly, but on some level I believe I resented her. Why did God give me this child and take away the one I'd loved so much?

Unable to adequately care for her, I handed over much of the workload to my husband. He wasn't exactly the mothering type, but he did the best he could. He fed her, changed her diapers, and comforted her when she cried. I could do little but grieve uncontrollably.

My husband, on the other hand, seemed to do little but work. He poured himself into his job. I believe I resented this, as well. I've since discovered that we all have our own ways of coping with pain.

Over a period of about six months I cried at the drop of a hat. I remember wondering if my husband ever grieved; I never saw him cry. I was told years later that he cried much during that first year. He just handled his tears privately. I also learned that he struggled with a tremendous amount of guilt. There are a lot of "if onlys" when you lose a child.

Of course, I grew to love that little newborn. In many ways, Connie turned out to be the sweetest, best behaved of all our children – and certainly the least demanding. The Lord, in his grace and mercy, blessed me with that little angel.

My husband and I went on to have two more children in later years – another girl we named Karen and finally a little boy we named Robbie. All four of our children grew up into men and women we're very proud of.

But that doesn't mean I've forgotten about Billy. No one could ever replace him. Over forty years have passed since his death. To this day, I still get a lump in my throat and tears in my eyes when I see a picture of that beautiful face or hear someone mention his name. He was, and always will be, my first-born. He was a beautiful gift from God – and will not be forgotten, regardless of the passage of time. – Shirley Moseley (as told to her daughter, Janice Thompson)

Love Remains
By Janice Thompson

If that which was taken
Has left you shaken
And bruised
And wondering,

Or questioning
The Giver of
Good News
Look up,
For He loves you
His heart breaks too
Through grieving
And sorrow
He shares the pain
That you
Will give to Him
Place in His hands
In pieces small
Or far too large
To bear
Don't give in to fear
Or doubt His care
His love…
That has not changed
For love remains
Steady, strong…
Beyond the pain

Shirley Moseley *resides in Texas and is active in her local church. She is the mother of five children, (including "Billy" mentioned in this story). Shirley loves her children, grandchildren and great-grandchildren very much, and believes in leaving a legacy. One way she accomplishes this is through her various quilting projects.*

Janice Thompson *is a Christian author from Texas. She has four grown daughters and a precious granddaughter. She and her daughters are active in ministry, particularly the arts. Janice is a writer by trade, but wears many other hats. She previously taught* *drama and creative writing and directed a drama ministry. She directs the elementary department at her church and enjoys public speaking. Janice is passionate about her faith and does all she can to share it with others.*

Charlotte's Comments

Just as God never forgot His first born, a mother never forgets hers. God gave this mother other children, but Billy will forever be in her heart. We will never forget any of our children God blessed us with. However, we learn to place them in His care until we see them again. One thing we can remember is: He loves them more than we do for He created them.

Sometimes the death of a child leaves a mother or father paralyzed for a time, as it did Shirley, but God is there and brings them through if they look to Him. If you are there, don't stay in that paralytic state. Let God bring you out to live again. Give your paralysis to Him and trust His love for you. He gives love strong enough to see you through and bring you out. It's your choice.

Prayer: *Lord, thank You for Your unfailing love and faithfulness. Helps us to go on when the storms of life paralyze us. Thank You for new life and hope. Continue to guide us and show us the good memories. Thank You for the love that remains true forever. Wrap us in Your* *arms of love when life stymies us. In Jesus Name. Amen.*

Chapter Thirteen
Gone In An Instant
By Millie Watson

We had recently moved from the city to a country farmhouse. We thought the country would be a good place to raise our two boys, Jay and Jimmy.

It was a beautiful day in May one week after my child, Jimmy's, sixth birthday. I gave him permission to go across the street to play with the neighbor children. He ran down the hill to the edge of the highway and stood waiting by the side of the road to cross. A car drove by very fast and caught Jimmy with his right headlight. I saw him rolling down the road, as I took my wash down from the clothesline. I ran as fast as I could. I thought I could catch Jimmy and save him lots of injuries. He stopped rolling underneath the mailbox. I couldn't believe it happened so quickly or that a life could be taken away in an instant.

Losing a child is one of the saddest things a parent has to handle. It's as though the whole world has crushed in upon you. Especially, when it is unexpected, as I experienced. It was more than I could bear. At least I didn't think I could bear it. But with God's help I was able. *No temptation has overtaken you except such as is common to man; but God is faithful, who will not allow you to be tempted beyond what you are able, but with the temptation will also make the way of escape, that you may be able to bear it.* 1 Corinthians 10:13 (NKJV)

I could not even think about it for some time. However, after we lost our Jimmy, I really felt the presence of God comforting me. I felt like a great big weight came off my shoulders. At the same time, out of the window I could see where his accident happened on the highway. I would envision him rolling down the hill, his body going down so fast.

The extended family and friends stood beside us and lifted us up during our time of grief, especially for the funeral. The attendance for Jimmy's service was overwhelming along with the beautiful flowers and the many expressions of love from everyone. However, people seemed to forget within a short period of time and go on with their lives. I continued to hurt and could have benefited from a friend's listening ear or a shoulder to cry on in the months ahead.

The mourning was still so strong. It even affected my health. I found myself unable to sleep. I broke out in a rash. I developed severe migraines. I felt I would not live very long. At the same time, I had the good sense to think I must go on for my other son, Jay, and my husband, James, for everyone. I couldn't be cowardly and selfish and not go on. I thought of all the other people in the world who had to bear such tragedies and turned to the dear Lord in heaven for strength. I thought there was some reason for it, though what it could be I did not know since Jimmy was an innocent child and had done no wrong.

We all felt the loss. My dear husband, James, stood strong until one evening when he broke down. I felt the whole bed shake with his sobs and could hardly bear to see him so distraught.

My older son, Jay, became rebellious a couple of years later and wanted to quit school. I believe it was his own slow reaction to Jimmy's death. He didn't know how to deal with it. He was only twelve when Jimmy died. I wished many times we had gotten counseling for him. Our family didn't encourage counseling. Back then it wasn't used as much as today. We could have benefited. I wholeheartedly encourage families who lose a loved one to engage in therapy, especially young children.

We never forgot Jimmy. He remains forever in

our hearts. We think of him daily. Time has proven to be a great healer, though it took many months before I could think about going on without him. Jimmy's death affected our lives very much. We knew we had lost a whole life. We did not see him start school. We didn't see him graduate or go to college. We would never know what his family would have been like. It was a huge loss, a big segment out of our life. I always came back to searching for some reason it had to happen.

Then, I think of other people who have had as much sorrow and loss as we have. Most people bear it and go through it with the help of our Lord Jesus Christ. He holds us up. His Spirit would say to mine, "He's in a good place now. He is taken care of."

Death is a fact of life. It is a hard thing but many go through it. Some of us learn to be compassionate toward other people because of the grief we have suffered. We learn to feel their loss when they have a terrible unexpected death like ours. I find I feel like more of a whole person. I can put myself in the place of another who has had the loss of a beautiful child.

I have learned to say the right words to people who have lost a child. Better than I ever did before I had the loss. I am fulfilled when I can comfort them. I feel so much stronger having gone through this tragedy. I can understand so much better someone else's sorrow. It is hard to explain but I feel so much at peace after so many years have passed. I think of him everyday and the wonderful memories I have. His father and brother feel the same way.

I did not get the blame for his accident. I feared I would but no one accused me ever. Not even a hint of blame, and for that, I am very grateful, other than what I placed on myself. Thankfully, my belief in my God and what the Bible tells me took away any blame. My son's death was something I just had to bear and I bore it with His help.

I need to carry on and enjoy a happy life and everything I have. All the beautiful things God gives us all around us – the blue skies, the birds that sing, the music we can listen to – all the wonderful things in the world.

I am really proud of all of us for having persevered in a very gainful way. It was the sensible thing to do. We had to be very strong. Getting down on our knees and praying helped bring us through. Talking to God and thinking of others, who are having hardships, makes our trials worthwhile. You know what they are going through. I am very thankful I have learned that.

Millie Watson *was born in the Upper Peninsula of Michigan but moved to Wisconsin at the age of two. As a teenager she was unable to graduate high school due to family finances, so at the age of 78 she went back and got her diploma. She is a widow and was married for 57 years. Millie has one other son, two grandsons and four great grandchildren. She has traveled extensively and now resides in Kingwood, Texas.*

Charlotte's Comments

The death and loss of a child takes its toll on our bodies. Grief can be so strong it affects even our physical health. We must rely on Him for our bodily strength as well as our spiritual strength. He uses doctors, exercise, good food, rest and, yes, counseling to bring about good health for our bodies and gives us the will to take care of them.

These types of tragedies can help us grow stronger emotionally and spiritually. It can help us minister to others. Before we can reach out to others, we must rely on God to help us. Without His strength we really have nothing to offer anyone else of lasting value. Other things, counseling and psychology can help but often it only puts a band aide on the pain without Him. God gets to the heart of the pain. Sometimes He uses these other methods to bring the needed healing but be assured - lasting hope and value comes from Him.

He truly wants us to comfort others as He has comforted us if we allow Him to use us. When we turn inward in our pain, we become stuck. Often times, we become bitter. We find ourselves in the middle of a pity party.

On the other hand, when we think of others, we turn outward and it not only helps others but us as well. If we focus on the help we can give to others, we tend to forget about our own suffering.

Millie made one point that struck my heart. We need to continue to lift up, encourage and be aware of a hurting parent(s) long after the funeral. The hurt and pain they experience does not erase itself when their child is buried. They need time to heal. They need someone to listen and hold their hand for months and maybe even years to come. I know there are organizations to aid them in this process but there is nothing like a dear friend they know and trust to help them over these humps. Let's be a friend to another hurting parent.

Prayer: *Lord, help us to turn outward rather than inward. Help us to reach out to those around instead of focusing on our own pain and ourselves. Help us to stop* *any pity party we might be having. We ask that You give us new strength in our bodies to glorify You. Thank You for taking away the pain and heartache. We release it to You. In Jesus Name. Amen.*

Chapter Fourteen
Forever Changed
By Fern Finley

October 19, 1948. A precious son, Milton Dene, was born. He was our third child. Charlotte Lorraine was our first and Ronald Eugene our second. Later, another son, Darrell Lyn was born. We were truly blessed by the Lord to be given four wonderful children.

Dene's October birthday would make him a year behind his friends in school. We enrolled him in a private school with the understanding that if he passed with good grades, he would be moved to the same class as his friends. He not only passed, he excelled.

One day, while praying, I had a dream or vision of losing one of my children. I saw a casket in the funeral parlor but could not tell which child lay inside. I became frightened and depressed. I told the dream to my pastor and husband. They assumed I was overly tired and upset so they prayed for me.

Some friends planned a week's vacation for their family at Dam B Park near Jasper. We reserved a campsite next to them upon their recommendation. I prepared breakfast there one morning while a group of children (including my four) played close to the water's edge. To my shock and horror, the dam opened and the undercurrent pulled the children away but Dene, our nine year old, was the only one pulled under. He reached for Ron, his brother, but his hand slipped off Ron's wet body. We never blamed Ron for Dene's death. Even though, I think at times, he did.

When we lost Dene, we remembered my vision/dream from years before. I suppose the Lord had either been warning or preparing us. Everything happened just the way I saw it. The casket had a glass encasement - the reason for my not knowing which child I saw in the vision.

My husband, Carl, and I were so caught up in our grief; it was as if it were a nightmare. The Lord and the Holy Spirit helped us go through the motions of our daily lives: at work, in the family and in the church. Our bosses were understanding and kind. They helped us walk through our grief.

Charlotte, Ronnie and Darrell were also grief stricken. We could have been helped with a good Christian counselor during that time. We struggled to survive and keep the family together even when it felt as if we were coming apart at the seams. God remained good and faithful all the time. He was our help in time of need – and we surely were in need during those years.

To lose a child is the worst thing to happen to parents, and to the siblings. It changes everyone's life forever. For the parents – sometimes the guilt of how to have prevented the tragedy, and for the children – why them and not me? For us, these seemed to be the questions we asked. The role each one plays in the family changes. The older feels responsible for the younger children and worries about how his parents feel. For Carl, the head of our home, to come out and say that Dene was gone was unbearably hard for all of us. My thoughts were: G*one where? Did someone take him somewhere else?*

The youngest child Darrell felt like he had to entertain and keep the mood in the home light, to take away Mom and Dad's pain. The middle child stayed at the camp for a while and wandered around. Maybe that was his coping skill. I often wondered how he felt about everything and if he thought it could have been him. He was able to get out. I knew he was probably scared, sad and confused because I was.

The family was forever changed by Dene's death. Carl and Dene shared an October birthday, so each year thereafter, it was a sad month. August was another sad month for us because Dene died then. We didn't ever want to take another vacation in August because we were afraid something like that could happen again.

At times I wonder how Dene would have looked as an adult. What occupation would he have? Would he like fine detail work like Daddy and Darrell? How would his children look? What kind of a wife would he choose? Would he be like Darrell and me, single in our older years? A lot of questions run through my mind. One thing I know - I miss him, as I'm sure all the family does.

A family never gets over losing one of its members. Everyone heals their own way and in their time, as they allow the Comforter to do His work in their lives. We are still being healed forty years later by the power of the Holy Spirit. Yes, the only way we are able to manage our grief is through trusting Him. I pray you will trust Him in your grief.

Fern Finley Langford is the mother of four. Her three living children make her proud. She has been a Missionary in Belgium, France, Germany, Scotland and Mexico. She was blessed to have married two Finley's. Both have gone on to be with the Lord. They were not related except in Spirit. Fern enjoys a large family with her own children, grandchildren, and great grandchildren along with stepchildren, their children and children's children. She has a quiver full. She resides in Kingwood, Texas.

Charlotte's Comments

I would have to agree with Fern. Once you lose a child you are never the same again. You may not be better or worse in many areas, but you are forever changed. I do pray we all will be better in some ways: We can now have empathy for others who have experienced this loss. We learn from whence comes our help. We rely on the strength of our God. We appreciate those we love and who love us. We give thanks for the time we had with our child. We cherish any other children we may have. We learn to trust Him in our grief.

This list could go on but I believe I made my point. I pray we will be better and stronger than ever before.

Prayer: *Lord, we thank You that we are not the same any more. We thank You that You have made us stronger and closer to You. Thank You for our precious loved ones. Thank You for helping in our time of need. Thank You, Lord, that we can trust You in our grief. In Jesus Name. Amen.*

Chapter Fifteen
Judith Suzanne
By Kay Holt

"Dear God, thank you for all the blessings, and forgive me for all my sins. Please let John's promotion come through, and help me make the dean's list again this quarter. Bless the sick and needy. My children! Please, please..."

Those words were typical of my daily prayers. They became passionate when I petitioned Him for my children's welfare. Joey was twelve years old and Judith, ten. Judith seemed the healthier of the two, although both were normal, bright children. We tried for ten years to have another child but assumed it not to be. I searched for reasons why things happened as they did, never considering God's timetable.

When Judith became slightly ill with a bad cold during the Christmas holidays, I was not too alarmed until her cold seemed to hang on. Soon I noticed a subtle change in her. She became pale, listless, not her usual high-energy self.

My memory remains vivid of the uneasy feeling

I felt - something didn't seem right. In fact, it scared me so, I wouldn't let my mind go there. Most parents know, the mere thought of something seriously wrong with our precious child takes us places we can't allow our thoughts to go and still keep our proper perspective.

Christmas came and went. The New Year brought tests and different drugs prescribed by the doctors, but nothing changed, except Judith became weaker. The fear of my life came to fruition when Dr. Guilfoil called us into his office for Judith's diagnosis: Acute Leukemia!

"Judith will not live more than a year at most." the doctor explained. "She can be given drugs to cause the disease to go into remission. Then she will appear normal until those drugs became ineffective." He carefully warned us not to get our hopes up. She was going to die.

I felt too stunned to pray, or even think, when I heard his diagnosis. I simply looked at the pictures on the doctor's wall as he explained the gravity of her condition. I nodded or shook my head, not actually responding to his words. The only rational thought I remember was my concern for him and the horrible duties doctors have to perform. *How can he bear telling me my child is going to die, and soon?* I looked from his wall paintings back to him. *Poor man.*

I sat composed for a time, hardly aware my husband dealt with the news in his own way, yet, he continually looked at me. So did the doctor. *Let us help you*, their eyes pleaded. I shook my head, motioning for them not to touch me. Who knew why? I learned later of the dreadful things going on in my husband's mind. He worried about whether or not we could bear such a thing, in our own strength, and go where this would take us.

A few minutes passed and Dr. Guilfoil asked, "Do you have any questions?"

I shook my head again. *He wants us to leave so he can forget about this part of his job. He knows this is too much for us to bear and remain sane. Is he going to ask me who the President of the United States is?*

"If it means anything," he added, "I just lost my mother with cancer."

"YOUR MOTHER! YOUR MOTHER?" I almost rose from the chair. Then I slumped back, hardly aware of my obstinate tone as I shook my head and almost whispered, "I could lose everyone I've ever known in my entire life more easily than I can give up my child." The words came from the innermost part of my psyche.

Desperation gripped me for days and I remember little of what went on. And that was all right. None of us spoke of anything beyond the moment. Tomorrow held its own horrors.

People came to visit us. Of course they grieved for us and wanted to help. I envied them, and everyone else, because they weren't all in the process of dying as we were. Christians always talked about God and His power. He could give me peace. They pleaded but those were words.

How can they suggest peace is possible for me without my daughter? Don't other people love their children as I love mine? Maybe not.

I was hardly rational about anything except my interaction with Joey. I worked hard to avoid telling him the gravity of Judith's illness. Of course, he became sad and confused because of her terrible sickness but we didn't talk about where it would take us. Not then, anyway.

Judith was admitted to the hospital and placed on steroids. She responded well. Immediately she began to eat and grow stronger. People came and went at our house, trying to encourage us. *How presumptuous.*

141

Do they really think I can be helped by anyone? My husband was hospitable and I'm sure he made excuses for my lack of graciousness. I remember an evening when our

Pastor, along with other church friends came to visit and pray. We all stood in a circle as each person prayed aloud.

I remained silent as I listened superficially to their hollow words. I wanted to scream. "My child is dying!" *Doesn't anyone understand there can be no peace for me?* I didn't even try to pray.

Today, I thank Him because these Christians were undaunted by me. They kept imploring God to give me peace. They never stopped what I considered "bothering" me.

Once during this time an idea occurred to me. *If You're really there, God, let this all be a mistake. Let me wake up from this nightmare. Please.* I started thinking the doctors were not all knowing. Perhaps they'd made a mistake in their diagnosis and would eventually realize it. Even the smallest chance of such a blunder excited me.

Later, when I approached Dr. Guilfoil with such a possibility, he looked at me with his familiar sadness.

"I wish it were true, but it's not the case."

Every day I stayed in Judith's hospital room, sitting constantly with my beautiful little blonde haired girl. We talked and I allowed her to think everything was fine, until I could find a way to deal with it. She was so bright, so sensitive! Of course I never let her see me cry but when I left her room, I lost control. The combination of rage and grief took over again and I vacillated between those emotions for weeks.

At home we existed. We ate, slept, and we talked - rarely. Then one day a few weeks following Judith's diagnoses, I found myself home alone. My husband worked at the office, Joey attended school and Judith lay in the hospital. All her reports turned out good. She entered remission and could come home soon. *To live a few months - at most, I reminded myself.*

On this particular day, I went into Judith's room and tidied up her dolls, her scrapbook and her school notes. Then I walked to her closet, opened the door and looked at her things. I reached out my arms and encircled all her clothes. I gathered and drew them to me. I buried my face in the material, which smelled of her sweet little body. I sobbed for a while.

Trusting Him In Your Grief/Charlotte Holt

An awareness distracted me and something about me changed. I couldn't define the difference. *What is it I need to know? Have I gone mad?* I stopped crying; aware my mood had become altered. *Why?* I looked around, searching for an answer and impulsively left Judith's room. I walked from room to room, almost with urgency. *I'm alone or am I? The doors are locked. Nothing's changed. Yet, something is bidding me. What?*

Finally I opened the door of a guest bedroom, not knowing why, because the room was rarely used. Then I walked straight to the bed, without purpose, and knelt there. My cheek fell against the cool spread, where my tears poured. It came so natural for me to whisper or think, *Lord, I cannot do this alone. Please…*

At that second my total being became engulfed by a presence so overwhelming I didn't need to speak or think further. I stayed there for several seconds, probably minutes, so aware of His exquisite embrace. Every cell in my body felt aware of *IT. This is God. This is what He is. Thank you, my Heavenly Father. You're wonderful. I'm all right. I can bear it now. Whatever is ahead, I will praise You eternally for this revelation of Yourself.*

I didn't speak aloud, but the outpouring of His love and the catharsis of my pent-up soul made me know

He was the answer. I would not be alone again. Finally, I arose and backed out of the room, aware that I would never be the same. The anguish, which previously gripped me, disappeared. He carried my grief.

I'm not sure about a light in the guest room where He met me. I don't think so. I didn't hear an audible voice. But, I felt His presence. Nothing could have enhanced or diminished the experience. I left the room, hugging my arms across my breast, savoring the newness of His Spirit that filled my heart with joy.

Soon Joey and John came home. I met them with the news of how God changed me. They'd never seen me like this. We all laughed, played and celebrated His Presence. We'd lived in a vacuum of misery for such a long time. Their lives changed too. From that day forward, our home was not the same. God resided there and He went with us every step of the way!

I comforted those friends, who previously tried to help me. My prayers now included thanksgiving and praise - instead of enumerating all the ways God could please me.

The people, who continued to pray for us, witnessed the power of their prayers by the change in us. Some rejoiced; others stood amazed and some were perplexed.

"Does Katie understand her daughter is terminally ill? Poor lady. Are we sure she's all right?" Some said.

Our family's best times occurred during the following months because God lived in the hearts of the four of us.

Judith had complete remission from the disease. Anything she wanted to do, we did if we could. We made ordinary things an adventure because we were high on God. There were doctor's appointments at least three times a week at first. These were special times too as we drew closer than ever to Him. Judith's blood was drawn constantly, yet, she never complained, not ever. She drew her own blood a few times and we laughed about her being so much braver than her mother. The doctors and nurses adored her.

During one of our visits, early on, we chatted with Dr. Guilfoil and his nurses.

At a quiet moment, a loud noise erupted from my stomach. Everyone glanced at me. I turned red and Judith giggled. Dr. Guilfoil stopped and looked in my direction. "How long has this been going on, Katie?" He looked at me for several seconds without blinking.

"I don't know," I said with a shrug. I wanted to ask, what's the big deal? But I respected him too much. "I haven't thought about it, Dr. Guilfoil," I added, squirming around on the sofa, a bit embarrassed. "Maybe a few weeks. Every morning, after orange juice, my stomach is in a turmoil, not bad, but noisy." Everyone laughed except him.

Judith was busy with the nurse and he motioned with his eyes for me to follow him down the hall. We stopped at the fountain. I asked, my voice barely audible, "What's wrong? What are you thinking?"

"I'm thinking you might be pregnant."

How presumptuous! He's dear to me. He's even cried with me and even spent time off duty with us, but this is too much.

"You must be joking. You know my children were born when I was a teenager. I've not been able to become pregnant since Judith."

"Have you missed a period?" His question was direct.

"Hummm…I don't know. I've been so busy…with Judith…"

His eyes were misty, as he spoke ever so gently. "I've seen this happen so many times in my practice.

Often when God takes one child, He sends another. Don't be surprised if you're pregnant. "

"Not this time, Doctor!"

"Will you go for a checkup? I'll make the arrangements for you to see my friend and colleague right now—just down the street."

He motioned with his head.

"I will think about making an appointment but I don't want to see the doctor right now," I said. We argued about my doing it now or later. Finally, I agreed to see the other doctor. He went to the phone, called his friend and told him my situation. His friend wanted me in his office in thirty minutes.

With Judith running beside me, we treated this idea as a joke. We rushed into the new doctor's office, a block away, and found ourselves ushered through a room full of very pregnant ladies.

"This is absurd. I can't believe I'm doing this." I murmured.

Judith became ecstatic. "I can't either. I didn't even pray for a baby brother or sister lately. But He knows I would like one." We'd recently chatted about all our answered prayers

I left the new doctor's office with Judith

skipping beside me, then in front of me, looking back at me.

"Oh, Mama, I hope it's a girl. But if it's a boy, I'll love him anyway. May I be first to tell Joey and Daddy? Huh?"

Spring passed and summer came and went. Judith swam and played with her girlfriends. She chose all my maternity clothes and was the first person, besides me, to feel the baby kick. It was hard to believe she wouldn't always be healthy. All too soon those months slipped away. By mid fall the drugs became ineffective. The evidence showed time running out for our precious little girl.

I prayed for her healing many times, asking God to make her well because I knew He could. At the time, I didn't understand His perspective on death and healing. I did know beyond a doubt He would see us through whatever might lie ahead. Of course, we were crushed but I accepted it early on and knew God would be with us.

I simply trusted Him and rested in the knowledge He would raise my precious child again. I learned in our guest room the day I *really* met Him that His total expression is love.

Many times during the darkest days, I slipped into that room again, seeking Him.

He always met me there and renewed my strength. He accompanied me every step of the way.

Judith and Joey's little brother, Stephen Carter, came into the world less than a month after she went to Heaven. When I started labor, God was so close. In fact, Stephen's birth was very easy. By His grace, my worries disappeared. I discovered it's possible to be completely broken hearted, and through it all, feel the peace of God.

Judith left us long ago. Both my sons are men now. Stephen heard all about his sister who adored him first, and he looks forward to seeing her one-day.

Joey, who resolved to become a scientist or a doctor in order to find a cure for the disease, which took his sister, is now a medical doctor. We rarely visit without talking about her. We reminisce how God, through her, changed all our lives forever. We will tell her about it one day, but I'm sure she had the full picture the day she went to be with Him.

Kay Holt was born in the hills of Tennessee. She received her undergraduate degree and attended graduate school in Atlanta, Georgia. Kay taught business English at Massey Junior College for twenty years. Through the years she wrote chapters for business textbook companies, did a weekly newspaper article for two years, was executive director of the chamber of commerce in Tennessee and authored a romance novel. She lives at present in metropolitan Atlanta, has two sons, four grandsons and one great grandson. Her only girl awaits her in heaven.

Charlotte's Comments

What a difference it makes when God comes into the picture. Things seem to totally change when we turn our lives and situations over to Him. When He touched Kay, all things changed.

He can, and wants to, do miracles in all our lives the way He did for her. Sometimes, it takes the hard trials of life for us to look to Him completely and confidently. When we let go of the things we hold on to, He replaces them with more than we can ever imagine.

No, Judith will never be completely replaced or forgotten but Kay released her to God's care. If you are holding on to anything or anyone, give it, or them, to God and experience the miracles He will give you.

The following poem by another author seemed to fit perfectly behind Kay's story of Judith Suzanne. Even though some of the other stories reflect some of the same feelings, I chose to place it here. We all know this emptiness. Yet, we know the joy of placing our child in the Father's hand, believing we will one day be together with them. All the pain will fade away as we experience the beauty of heaven and its eternal state. We will live forever with our child.

Prayer: *Lord, help us to release our children to Your loving care. Thank You for the miracles You do in our lives. I pray You will do a miracle of healing right now for those who are reading this book. Help all of us to give our grief and child over to You completely and confidently. In Jesus Name. Amen.*

Take This Kiss
By M. Saint Germain

My love and I, two lives—then one
Together, promised to love Him.
A seed unites. Miracle, birth,
We bend on our knees to thank Him.

Blissful days of a happy child
Sheltered and cocooned in our nest.
The joy, the fun, and the laughter
Fill family life with the best.

Stop. Times up. Borrowed gift is gone.
Darkness engulfs, swallows the dawn.
Where is our 'lil girl? Where are we?
Only raw, empty lives to see.

Alone are unfilled shoes and skates.
Lonesome girl toys beg for playmates.
Folded clothes left in drawer spaces.
Bicycles parked in dark, cold places.

Homework papers left un-graded.
Books on shelves with words now faded.
One dry toothbrush cold and cheerless.
Hearts once filled now hollow, childless.

Brushes, bows with torn blonde tresses,
Pink and purple party dresses,
Silent, waiting, 'lone in the dark.
Frowning swings glide in vacant park.

No bare footsteps in the hallways

Trusting Him In Your Grief/Charlotte Holt

Running from storm's lightening rays.
No bear hugs or sloppy kisses
Or once-upon-a-star wishes.

Crayon-drawn walls with empty cries
Won't hear the bedtime lullabies.
Quiet mealtimes with empty chairs,
Coats hung on hooks with open stares.

No homemade cards for Mother's Day
That mean far more than words could say.
No questions "may I drive tonight?"
That end in stubborn strong-willed fights.

No dance-filled high school spring prom dates
Or giving strong heated debates.
No sisters of sororities
Or college professors to please.

Empty church aisles, no bride and groom
No tears of joy and love to bloom.
Dreams are feathers, lost in a storm,
Carried away—shredded and torn.

Prayer.... More prayer.... Not a sound.
Where is He? Nowhere to be found.
Show us how to be strong like You.
Help us go on, understand, too.

We see it! Your love and Your light.
A blurred window—the unclear sight
Time—painful time, and trust in You,
Helps us comprehend all You do.

Peace and a smile. Hear Him. Rejoice.
Even though darkness gives no choice.

Trusting Him In Your Grief/Charlotte Holt

He has her, we had, she's His now.
We go on—'though we don't know how.

Above, in His place, now will be
Our daughter that we used to see.
The love and trust in His mighty grace
Will continue in her one-time place.

We'll shine as we remember
And thank him for bringing her—
From His love so pure and deep
To our hearts, then His to keep.

But, this borrowed gift in our lives,
Will never leave our hearts or eyes.
Instead, we'll remember her grace
And the beauty, her smiling face.

Dear child, may you rest your pale head
On the pillows of heaven's bed.
Let there be no pain or despair
For you'll always be in His care.

With His soft and gentle hands
He'll protect you from the dark.
We'll join you when He calls us—
When it's our blessed turn to part.

Take comfort in knowing we'll come.
We'll follow light, His only son.
Please pray, be patient while you wait.
Trust in His holy, loving fate.

Take this kiss from mommy and me.
Put it in your pocket, safely.
Be His sweet angel until then—

'Til we are together again.

*M. **Saint-Germain** is a YA author and blogger at Random Writing Rants, Teaching Adults and Teens How To Get Published. Her current wips include: The Muggler, Willow, Love is Just a Word, Kelly's Story, and The Vision in a Kiss. She's been published in Adoptive Families, Brio Magazine, Church Libraries, Kyria, The Writer's Digest and has won contests in both The Writer's Journal and The Writer's Digest. Besides writing she's a tennis junkie, book slut, and a fun-loving Mimi.*

Chapter Sixteen
It Was Not God's Will
By Susan Jones

January 6, 1993, began as a typical day for me. I was general manager of a medium-sized local real estate franchise and dealt with the day's challenges, meeting each one with my usual mixture of common sense, humor and enthusiasm. I was in a meeting with our District Manager, Margaret, discussing my goals for the company when someone knocked on my office door, daring to completely ignore my "Don't Even Think About Disturbing Me" sign. The gentleman sheepishly opened the door and said, "There's an emergency call for you on line one." I don't know why, but I glanced at the clock and noticed it was 4:00 in the afternoon.

The voice of my ex-husband, Rich, filled my ear as I answered the phone. He told me our son, Matt had been shot and I needed to go to the house as quickly as possible. I hung up the telephone, laid my head on my desk and began sobbing uncontrollably. Margaret tried to comfort me, as did several of the staff present. It was as if they all knew this was more than the typical childhood emergency.

One of the agents drove me to the house while

another tried to locate my husband, Chuck. I could see an ambulance and several police cars in front of my home as we drove up the street. There were children standing around crying with a few adults trying to comfort them. A policeman stopped me from going into the house as I ran up the driveway. He told me my son had been shot in the head and the paramedics were working on him. I almost collapsed right there.

Chuck arrived at that time and held me while we waited. Then I saw them wheeling my son down the driveway on a gurney. When I approached, I could see Matt was not conscious but I pressed my hands to his and spoke to him anyway. I guess something deep inside me wanted to let him know I was there. He was going to be life-flighted to Herman Hospital so I asked someone to call his father and stop him from coming all the way from Houston and divert him instead to Herman.

When we arrived at Herman, a surgeon told us Matt had been shot in the back of the head from the right side. The bullet exited through the left temporal region. He said Matt was strong and healthy and he wanted to operate to repair the damage. He assured us he would not consider operating if he thought Matt would be left paralyzed or worse and encouraged us by saying Matt had a good chance of returning to normal.

By the time Matt came out of surgery many hours later, we had called together all of the prayer warriors we could muster. Many came to the hospital and sat vigil with us throughout the long days that followed. Even our pastor stayed with us, turning his services over to the Associate Pastor. Pastor Chris felt his place was with us at that time. We never stopped praying and we never stopped believing our son would return to us a normal, healthy young boy. Five days later he died.

Matthew Carmen Negri was born March 7, 1979. He was healthy and beautiful and full of life as are most babies. He was the fourth of four sons in our blended family. We could tell from the beginning that Matt was unusually smart so we entered him into a Montessori school as soon as he was old enough. The local soccer team accepted him at the age of four.

When Matt was five years old, he came downstairs one morning and announced to his father and me, "Jesus visited me in my room last night!" It astounded us to hear this come from the mind of a five-year old but asked him to tell us about it.

"Jesus said He would use my hands to save

children and He has a message for you," Matt said. We encouraged him to continue and he said, "Jesus said to tell you that, no matter what happens, everything will be OK."

Now if you think that wasn't confusing, you're wrong! We couldn't even imagine what that meant. But Matt believed God was calling him to be a doctor; he just didn't know if he was supposed to deliver babies (become an OB/GYN) or take care of children (be a pediatrician). We told him God would show him what to do when the time came. Every day from that day forward, Matt set his sights on becoming a doctor.

He did well as a student and took his studies very seriously. But that did not make him a nerd or a geek. He was athletic, excelling in soccer and football. He was very popular with both boys and girls. They voted him 'Most Athletic' in his eighth grade class. The previous summer, Matt traveled to France with the State soccer team, The Texans, to compete on an international level. The Texans placed third - in the World! They won over several European and South American teams. We were so proud of them. The following summer they signed up to compete in Russia and Matt looked forward to it with eager anticipation.

During his eighth grade year, Matt told his dad and me that he wanted to go to Baylor College of Medicine.

"OK," we said, "but you have lots of time to decide that."

"No, you don't understand. I want to go to Baylor now so I can visit with the counselors and find out what I need to do in high school to make sure I get into medical school."

We almost fainted. But, Matt set his sights on obediently following God's plan for him to become a doctor and nothing was going to get in the way. So we made plans to take him to Baylor when school let out that year. Only by that time, Matt was no longer with us.

Many people tried to make us feel better by saying things like, "It was God's will." Or, "You have other children to think about." Or, "You just have to get over it and go on."

How wrong they all were. *It was not God's will!* We already knew that God's will for Matt - and for all of us - is to lead "a happy, prosperous, healthy life to the fullness of our days" (paraphrased). We know Satan is the one who comes "to steal and kill and destroy." Satan is the father of lies and the one thing he wants you and me to believe is that "God did this."

Well, if you believe that, Satan wins. God does *not* want us to be sick or diseased and He does not want our children to die. He wants only what is best for us - all the time. And it is up to us to stand on His Word when Satan tries to take away God's promises.

So then you can ask, "what about Jesus visiting your son when he was five - what about that prophesy?"

Well, I believe that what Satan intended for evil, God turned to good. You see, we donated Matt's organs - to save the lives of children!

I knew that my son knew Jesus. More intimately than I think most people ever get to know Him in this life. But it was blessed news when two of Matt's camp counselors from the previous summer wrote to me to tell me that Matt received Jesus as his personal Lord and Savior that summer. I know where my son is today and I know that I will see him again.

After a few months of wallowing in self-pity, I awoke one morning to hear (not audibly of course) the Lord calling me into service. And He didn't make it easy. He didn't call me to an ordinary ministry or to join a prayer circle. He called me to become a chaplain down at the Texas Medical Center ministering to terminally ill children and their parents.

How could I let one child go, not knowing Jesus? How could I let one parent shrivel up in despair, not knowing if they would see their beloved child again? I could not. I did not. And through that ministry, God healed me of the pain and anguish in which I would have allowed myself to die.

At that same time, I began to accumulate all of the books I could find written by Christian parents who had lost children. I read books about God's love for me and began to study His Word diligently to see if I could find answers. God led me to a study of Heaven. What a blessing to know not only with whom my son is spending eternity but *where.* And Heaven is a very real place. I also listened to Christian music practically 24/7. I separated myself from those who told me it was God's will and I surrounded myself with uplifting Christian friends.

The pain became less as time passed and the beautiful memories became more comforting. No, he has not become Saint Matt to me. That would be a dishonor to his real spirit - the spirit of a wonderful, active, normal little boy whom God called - and then called home.

And what about God's promises to answer our prayers and heal us? Well, He did answer my prayers - my son is healed. And whole. And living in eternity with my Lord and Savior. Could I desire anything better for my son?

TWO ROADS
By Susan Jones

Two people traveled hand in hand
As they journeyed down life's road.
One was destined for boundless joy
The other for a heavy load.
They went as far as the Lord allowed,
Many battles to overcome.
But then they came to a fork in the road
This mother and her son.

"We've come to a fork in the road now, Dear,
And must travel our separate ways.
To me God gave the long and rough
To journey the rest of my days.
My road is steep and filled with ruts;
It won't be easy to travel alone.
I will be filled with doubts and pain
Till I reach my final home."

"But you, Dear Child, got the easy road
And rainbows you now see.
No more tears to wipe away
As you sit on your Father's knee.
No illness, poverty nor pain,
And golden streams now line your road.
Your way is bright and filled with love
While mine's a heavy load."

"But travel on I will, I must
And God has given me
A map to Heaven's pearly gates
Which, Matthew, you now see.
My road is long and sometimes steep
But His Word lights my way,
And knowing that you'll greet me there
Brings light to each new day."

"My prayer is that I live this life
And travel down this road
Loving, serving, keeping Him
In humblest abode,
So He will choose me on that day
When my road finally ends
And I may dwell with Him and you
Where no road ever bends.

Susan Jones resides with her husband, Chuck, in Roman Forest, Texas. Through the death of her beloved son, Mathew, Susan grew in strength, compassion and understanding of God's Word. She serves the Lord in whatever way He chooses. She and Chuck worked in refugee camps in Indonesia following the devastating tsunami. Building bridges with the Muslim people is the desire of her heart and they will return to Indonesia to continue their mission work. They lead the missions program at their church and have spearheaded many trips both at home and abroad.

Charlotte's Comments

How terrible it is when dreams are lost with the death of a child. This son held potential for greatness.

Like many others he could have become a leader of our nation, or at least one in his field. Whether or not a child has great potential, we still miss out on what they could have been when they are taken early in life. However, we only see a small part of the puzzle and God knows the whole picture.

Even though it may not have been God's will, we can trust that He will make the best out of these terrible circumstances. Susan acknowledges she has grown stronger through her trials and sufferings. She will never stop missing or longing for her child, like the rest of us, but God will be there to encourage, help, and sustain.

Prayer: *Father, help us to give our lost dreams to You and accept the ones You have for us. Thank You for sustaining us through the dark nights and the dreary days after our child's death. Thank you for encouraging and helping us in our time of need. Thank You for being there for us. Show us Your will and Your way for each of our lives. Thank You that we can learn to live again and grow stronger and more useful for Your Kingdom. In Jesus Name. Amen.*

Chapter Seventeen
The Rainbow
Anonymous

On a cold night in January, three police officers came to my door. They informed me of the death of my beloved children, Amanda and James. There was no warning, no preparation and no goodbyes. I still thank God my sister- in law, Mary, was with me, for without her presence I don't know what I would have done. I did not want to believe what the officers told me.

Amanda, a petite 16-year-old with beautiful auburn hair and striking blue eyes, was a comedian, headstrong, sometimes a drama queen and so vibrant. Recently in love for the first time, she looked radiant.

James was a skinny, seven year-old blond boy with a mischievous grin, who stayed in constant motion. He loved his kitten, Shelia, who was playful like him. He tried to tell jokes but usually forgot the punch line. He was proud of his new ability to read.

In one instant, my whole world became shattered. I never thought my children would die before me. It defies the natural order of things, even more so when children are murdered. The details of their deaths are very ugly. I have no words to adequately describe my shock, my horror and my grief.

How was this possible? Oh sure, we see these horrible things on television and in the news but they don't happen to you or to those you love. I considered myself a good mother, always watching out for my children's well being. I put locks on the poisons under the sink, safety plugs on the outlets. I made them buckle their seatbelts, taught them to look before crossing the road, warned them of strangers and so many other things.

My pastor once told me not to try and understand. That was good advice. One man made a choice. We all have choices to make. We can listen to our inner demons or we can turn to God. I could make no sense of this thing. Therefore, I left it with God.

The days following that night became a blur to me. I was not really there in many ways. I stumbled thru the funeral preparations in a state of disbelief. I think God lets us handle a very severe trauma in little bits and pieces.

I lived through the weeks and months following my children's deaths in a state of denial. I feared for my sanity because I did not believe this could be true. Yet, my heart knew it was. The grief felt real.

I remember the overwhelming guilt. Being their mother, it was my sacred duty to protect them. How could I let this happen? Guilt can destroy. I thought of all the occasions when I could have acted kinder towards my children. All the times I could have paid more attention to them. The hugs I didn't give. When I gave in to the guilt, I did self-destructive things. I drank too much, I didn't eat, or I slept for days. I quit caring about myself. I learned to be careful of those inner voices that told me to feel guilty.

I reminded myself that Jesus forgives us of all our sins. Whether the sin is real or imagined, we must forgive ourselves in order to go on. In Ephesians chapter six, Paul talks about putting on the armor of God. The truth is I would have died for my children. I loved them that much. This became my armor against the guilt.

I remember touching Amanda in her casket and feeling how cold she was and seeing how small James looked in his. It rained on the way to the funeral and I felt the heavens were crying with me. I remember sitting through the funeral feeling so cold and unable to stop shivering.

The music I picked for their service was for

them. James's favorite song played as tears rolled down my face. Amanda's high school choir sang and some of the children had tears rolling down their faces as they sang.

As the months passed I cried out over and over, "I just want them back." I cried because Amanda would never get her drivers license or go to the senior prom. I cried because James would never finish first grade. I cried because I would never hear him call me mommy again. I cried at the sight of his favorite cereal still in my pantry. I cried at the sight of the biggie fries at Wendy's that Amanda loved so much. I cried for all the things they would never do and the things we would never do together.

I realized we would never curl up on the sofa watching silly movies. We would not play in the park or go on vacation to the beach together. I cried for me. I was left here so empty and alone without them. I felt so old and used up. Why was I still here? They were so young and innocent. They were just children. They had so much to live for. I still cry.

I prayed, "God, please let me be insane so this won't be real."

I remember wanting to die because no one

could live with the pain I felt. I wasn't able to see how I could go on, yet I was unable to kill myself. I couldn't deny my belief in our Father by committing such an act. My mother had suffered so much at the loss of her grandchildren. How could I bring her more pain?

Looking back, I know it was the wondrous acts of kindness and love of my family and friends that helped me through. People I had never met sent me cards. The community helped with funeral expenses. Friends and neighbors brought food and support. Even strangers grieved with me over the loss of my children. They will never know how much it meant to me. Knowing so many other people cared; the world didn't feel quite so cold.

I have kept a journal for years, full of poems, ideas and stories. I became too busy and stopped writing several years earlier. Suddenly, just two weeks before my children passed away, I was stricken with the desire to write again. I scribbled some ideas. One idea in particular had the potential for an excellent poem. The poem was about not doubting God.

With all the things He had done in my life, how could I ever doubt Him? We had been going through a rough time but I knew God was there for me. Why did I forget all the wonderful things He had done?

These thoughts came back to me right away. I began to pray. I believe God prepared me to turn to Him in this time of crisis. I felt blessed that He had gently reminded me never to doubt Him.

One thing I knew; my children were with Him. He was their one true Father. This brought the only real peace I could find. I believe with all my heart that death is not the end. One day I will be with our Lord and my children again. This thought sustains me today. It is okay to grieve for my loss, but slowly I have to let go. I have not yet entirely let go of them. That is all right too. I give myself permission to take as long as I need.

During this time, a dear friend reminded me to keep praising God. In addition, another told me about Job. I remember praying that I not become an angry bitter person. Perhaps, I was helped by the fact that the man who did this also died. It's difficult to seek revenge on a dead man. However, mostly I never want to become anything remotely like him. A lot of people prayed for me and this brought me peace.

Even with this comfort, I needed more. A mother has a habit of worrying about her children. I wanted very badly to know that they were okay. I prayed constantly in the morning, during the day and at night. I couldn't make it through without His help.

One afternoon a few weeks after the funeral I was at my home with Mary. Everyone took turns being with me, I think they were afraid to leave me alone. My mother stopped by with some groceries. She also brought a pamphlet on grief. I had begun seeing a counselor and I already knew about the stages a person went through. I was in a particularly bad mood that day and had no desire to read any more about it.

However, I decided to pretend to look at the pamphlet for Mom's sake. It would be good to let her feel she was helping me. I skimmed through the booklet and one short paragraph caught my attention. It was about a gentleman who had lost his mother. One day while visiting her grave shortly after her death, he saw a rainbow. He mentioned that seeing a rainbow means your loved one is at peace. Well, I knew about the Biblical significance of a rainbow but I never heard that. I thought the story rather lovely and nothing more. I didn't mention this to anyone.

After Mom left, Mary and I talked awhile. I tried to write some thank you cards. Everyone had been so kind but I found the cards difficult to write. Mary was cooking in the kitchen when suddenly she wanted me to look at something. She sounded excited, so I got up to see.

When I entered the kitchen, the most magnificent rainbow I had ever seen appeared right out my back door. I knew instantly what this meant. I didn't have to think about it for even a second. My heart was overjoyed by the answer the Lord had sent me. A monumental weight lifted from my shoulders. I explained to Mary what this rainbow meant to me. She cried with me.

She noticed it was a spectacularly beautiful rainbow, but also it ended in the playground behind my house. My apartment was on the second floor and from the patio door in the kitchen we could see over a privacy fence and into the playground of a daycare. I had never before seen the end of a rainbow and I doubt I ever will again. The next day I recalled how vivid the colors had been.

Mary said that although it was winter when we looked at the rainbow the grass around it appeared very green to her - something I had not noticed. Today the grass was brown and dull again.

I believe the Lord speaks to us through prayer,

and dreams, and sometimes rainbows. When we ask, He answers. Sometimes they take awhile or we don't always like what we hear. Other times, we miss what God was trying to say.

I have learned to keep my eyes and heart open. He never forsakes us. I made it through the first year only half believing I could. Now, I know I can go on because through God all things are possible. Now, it is not enough just to go on. I have made choices. I choose to become a better person. Not to become bitter, but to go on with all the joy I can find. This is what He truly wants for me. I still cry and that is okay. Nevertheless, I smile, I laugh and I love.

I dream of a wonderful future, where I write children's stories, where I give my love to foster children, who need me. I know the most important thing in my future is that God will always be in it. Not just on Sunday, or when I need help, but everyday. For that is the greatest blessing of all, to finally have that kind of relationship with our Lord.

Charlotte's Comments

Children are murdered everyday. This doesn't make it any less traumatic, horrible, or unbelievable. How can anyone murder a child? We ask this question.

Yet, unborn babies, toddlers, young people, adults are murdered, some without mercy or without cause. This leaves parents to cope, or not, with their grief. It leaves some parents bitter but some get better, as Cindy describes in her story. This is a choice we all make. We can chose to let the death of our child make us a bitter and angry person or we can get better in spite of, or because of, their death.

Cindy learned several important keys to getting through her grief. She described them in her story. She went for counseling, accepted the love and help of others, remembered the good times with her children, pushed away any guilt feelings. She accepted the forgiveness of the Father, recognized her children would be with Him and went on with her life after a time. She sought for answers and knew she would someday see her children again.

She showed a willing and teachable spirit. She listened to the Word of God and what the Spirit of the Lord told and showed her. Most importantly, she felt secure in her relationship with her Lord and Master, Jesus Christ.

She has learned, like the rest of us that she can trust Him in her grief. He is a good God and remains so always. He takes us through the mountains, valleys, good and bad days, trials, joys, tribulations, mourning and rejoicing – all the time.

He delights in showing us His love through such miracles as the rainbow. He even puts things in our hearts, such as, "when it rained, it was as if God cried with me." What an awesome God we serve.

Prayer: *Lord, give each of us a willing and teachable spirit so we might listen to You. Thank You that we can feel secure in our relationship with You. Help us to develop a closer one so we might know You more, love You more, and be more like You. Thank You for being there at all times. In Jesus Name. Amen.*

Chapter Eighteen
Dawn Another Day
By Judith Ditrich

Car accidents, detectives resolve – national disasters, scientists explain. But, why our children die in our arms at young ages still remains a sorrowful mystery. A doctor signs the death notice with cause of death in plain view, yet the grieving parents want to know the complete answer.

This is an answer that will not come from any man. Life and death are God things. In our deepest sorrow then, we must draw ourselves close to Him and wait for His touch and revelation.

Until we hear from heaven it's as though we've entered a stage of pseudo-mummification. The trauma stiffens us like gold fish frozen in the bowl incapable of feeling anything but the cold around us. When this happens we must seek the fire of God's presence for warmth and life. His light must penetrate the death shroud of darkness that covers our soul. We must allow His Word and His Spirit to speak to our cold dry bones and command them, "Live!"

This is the truth the Lord led me through when

178

our first child, Dawn Marie was diagnosed with an aggressive malignant cancer at the age of 18. The entire illness and each diagnosis hit us like brutal cold waves upon hard rock trying to destroy us all. But, because of God's love and faithfulness we stood firm. Even as the flesh was taken away our Spirit's grew greater over compensating the loss. Throughout her days of suffering our spirits pushed our flesh around as we applied faith in God's Word.

Dawn had just graduated from high school. Beautiful, kind, intelligent, and fun loving, she was eager to attend college in the fall. She had excelled in her academic endeavors throughout the school years. We called her our joy girl because she always brought laughter and enthusiasm into our lives. Her hugs and kisses, smiles and tears all made their mark in our minds and hearts. From conception through graduation and everyday in between she wove herself into the fabric of our lives.

We remembered first teeth, first steps and first words. Each new experience was recorded within our hearts over 18 years. She became more than daughter. She was also a confidante, friend.

I watched her stumble across the stage at her

honors ceremony and a clenching fear gripped me that there was something more seriously wrong with her than a pinched nerve. She was put on crutches in mid June and by mid July was hospitalized due to increased pain. During that time she saw over 30 doctors who gave her a myriad of diagnoses and prescriptions. At the end of a two-week stay, an oncologist discovered a mass covering the lower abdomen.

At his request she made an appointment to be seen at M.D. Anderson in another two weeks. For some that meant miracles and healings but for Dawn it meant entering a realm of the macabre and torment. We went through hours of interrogation until a four-inch chart bound in metal was put together for her. We wheeled her from specialist to specialist where we encountered halved and scarred patients bandaged together and connected by tubes to machines that flashed and beeped periodically.

In every waiting room we closed our eyes and held hands and prayed for doctors and patients alike. We left tracts on tables to encourage others as we stood in faith for ourselves.

The specialists that saw Dawn told us at the first meeting that she would die. She had a rare form of cancer. They knew of only four cases and all of those patients died. My husband boldly asserted our statement of faith. The doctor coldly reiterated his verdict of death. He continued to do this every time he saw Dawn over the next months as she was hospitalized for surgeries, comas, transfusions and emergency visits.

The Lord was present to us through His Word and others that surrounded us during this time. Dawn kept a prayer journal and shared revelations with us as the Lord showed her things. She had an unshaken confidence in His divine purposes being accomplished for her life. He showed her what some of the patients needed.

"When I'm healed I will help them, not only with cures, but with changes in public areas for easier wheel chair accessibility and all," she often told us.

But recover she did not. All her beautiful hair fell out one day in a second. She cried for most of that day until I came in with a wig. When she put that on, even she had to laugh. Somehow we got it styled and she looked better. Most often though she'd wear her turban and pretend she was an Indian Princess.

At the end of three chemo treatments and numerous surgeries, doctors released her to home and hospice care. Even so our faith stayed firm.

Up to her eighteenth year all her new accomplishments were progressive and onward. With the discovery of the illness her achievements moved toward handling the challenges of regression and decline.

Things I once did for her as a child I was now doing over again – like bathing her and helping her to walk. I got up in the middle of the night and rubbed her back and legs and feet. Before the ordeal was over I learned how to catheterize her and clean her colostomy bag.

Over 400 churches around the world prayed for her. Faith filled anointed ministers sent prayer clothes. Pastors, preachers, prophets, evangelists and worshippers all visited and laid hands on her. The presence of the Lord was strong upon her. Others felt it in her room. Her face shined with His glory. She prayed for sick friends and rejoiced when they were healed.

Dawn's faith transcended this world and with spiritual eyes she saw people preparing for a party. She said it looked like a wedding. Her eyes often stared beyond this realm as she sensed His coming. She no longer waited for a healing. She longed for Him. He would ultimately come to her and steal her away like a Jewish husband coming at an unknown hour to take His bride.

By December 12, Dawn stopped talking. She slept almost constantly. I had a vision one day of my brother-in-law, who had died in May, rowing a boat out on a clear lake. It appeared as though he was going to get someone. I knew it was Dawn.

People continued to visit and pray for her. One lady had a vision of her perfectly healed and walking and dancing. I knew that was a confirmation of her in heaven soon.

On Friday, December 15, I went out to rake leaves while a visiting nurse tended her. My hands began to swell so I went inside and took off my rings. Among them was my mother's ring that held my birthstone and the birthstones of all six children in it. I never saw that ring again. Dawn has it in heaven.

We gathered her brothers and sisters and each one kissed her goodbye. Around three in the afternoon, my husband, my sister and I sat at the foot of the bed and read her the twenty-third Psalm. During the reading Dawn lifted her arms and said, "I love you, Jesus."

In the Spirit, I saw her come up out of a clear

lake dressed all in white. Jesus ran to meet her and lifted her up in his arms and ran with her through a beautiful meadow.

One by one pastors and friends began to call us. Many came over. The doctor called an ambulance to verify her death. Then he came and signed the death certificate. Dawn's friends came and sat in her room until the hearse arrived. They laughed and cried but mostly laughed because she had left some of heaven's joy behind and no one was deeply saddened.

The first hearse was in an accident and another didn't come for two hours. Dawn would have liked the delay, just to have her friends together for a while longer. In the kitchen songs of praise were sent up to God. Divine occurrences continued in our home.

Dawn had to be moved to the chapel at the funeral home for more room. Flowers and people pushed their way in as hundreds came to pay their respects. The morning of the funeral the worship leader said he felt compelled to change his opening song. He opened with Psalm 23.

During the service our five-year old son saw an angel at her casket all dressed in gold and looking radiant. Later during the holidays I found a small angel dressed in gold and bought it to serve as a constant reminder of what he had seen.

It snowed a few days after her burial and the ground was covered with white. This wouldn't be too unusual if we lived in the north but in south Texas snow is not common. A friend informed me of a saying among the Indians: When it snowed after a death, it was a sure sign the person had entered heaven.

We definitely felt heaven's touch but then again we were looking for it. We passed nothing off as coincidence. We were assured our loving Father intervened to bring us peace and comfort.

Ever since the fall of man, humans have suffered and died. We have often attempted in vain to explain why such awful things happen to us. Even the best explanations seem hollow when compared to the severity of our losses. Our manmade assumptions are often like bandages we apply to try and hold ourselves together when tragedy strikes.

We search for reason frantically within all the unreasonable events that blow into our lives and shatter our souls. Teachers tell us they are for learning. Philosophers say they are for changing. Theologians propose they are punishment or discipline from a loving

Father who is trying to perfect us. Very simplistically, preachers shout, "It's the devil's doing!"

Mourners are supposed to find relief from all these so-called answers that will bring comfort, understanding and peace. The truth is, even if we do accept any of these hypotheses, there is still a part of us in which an unresolved question mark holds its place. What seems so clear and certain to others still remains clouded and uncertain to the wounded soul.

God gave me a vision during praise and worship one day. I saw Dawn ice skating on a beautiful crystal lake. She was dressed in white and wore a peach rosebud flower lei around her neck. She looked radiant. That week I found a little musical angel. She wore a white robe decorated in peach rosebuds. Of course, she went home with me and took her place alongside the gold angel.

Every time I see a wheel chair ramp or see how sidewalks have been adjusted to accommodate them I think of Dawn's desire and wonder if somehow she pulled strings in heaven.

I was really shocked one night while watching the news. Dawn's specialist was being interviewed. Someone in the hospital had been healed of the very same cancer he said there was no cure for. Even though it had happened, he was still hesitant to believe it because it had never happened before. My husband and I looked at each other then looked up to heaven. Simultaneously we said, "Dawn!" and smiled. Miracles are sent from heaven after all.

The Word of God tells us to store up treasures in heaven. We know, Dawn, one of our most treasured possessions is there. We do miss her a lot but we are assured our separation is not permanent. With every morning sunrise we are confident we will meet our Dawn another day.

Judy Ditrich held the office of President and Vice-President/Program Chairman for Humble Inspirational Writers Alive! The Bullard Weekly News recently published "The Making of a Patriot," a poem Judy wrote for her son when he joined the Marine Corps. This poignant tribute also appears in IWA!'s anthology, Inspirations. Judy has completed a Study Guide for The Healing Leaf, a book written by her pastor. She enjoys writing when she can get a quiet moment. Journaling is a favorite pastime and often, as her thoughts turn toward God, home and family, a poem, essay or short story may result.

Charlotte's Comments

What pain Judy and Norm must have experienced watching their child go down hill. However, this family never lost their faith and hope in the Lord.

They kept the faith in the tough times. I know the family personally and know they have a love for God that extends beyond human reason.

Many parents watch their children suffer and die. I hope they will be able to have a measure of faith like Judy and her family's. They are an inspiration to all those around. Judy continues to wear a smile on her face in the midst of whatever circumstances she finds herself.

Her very presence exudes the love and compassion she shows for others. She and her husband, Norm, are a joy to be around. They stay ever mindful of others and their needs. You can tell they walk daily with their Lord and Master, the Lord Jesus Christ.

Prayer: *Lord, I pray we will all show forth Your presence by our very presence. May we be mindful of the needs of others. Help us to walk daily with You. Be with those parents who suffer such painful losses by experiencing a child's prolonged illness. May they have a faith that will carry them through. Let us be an inspiration to all those around us. In Jesus Name. Amen.*

Chapter Nineteen
He Will Carry You Through
By Cecelia Trivitt

My love for the Lord has brought me through numerous valleys and allowed me to experience many mountaintops. I would like to share some of them.

In 1957 we were blessed with a beautiful eight-pound baby boy named Carey Lynn. He was delivered by cesarean section, which created a problem for him. Some of the anesthetic entered his blood stream and he developed pneumonia. He lived for only ten days. We were so devastated and hurt, but I felt then, and still feel, there might have been health problems later on in his life and God spared him the pain.

Many times since then, I have wished my relationship with God at the time, was what it is today. I could have handled my pain so much easier. Often times, we turn our burdens over to Him only to take them back in a few minutes, thinking God isn't fast enough. We think we can do a better job. We constantly need to remind ourselves that He is in control and His answers are in His Word.

We had two more lovely children, Janelle and

189

Jeffrey. In raising them, more and more we realized how important God is in our lives. We found answers in His Word as we grew stronger in His love and we learned to pray for His guidance in everything.

The births of our children were our mountaintop experiences followed by the evening Janelle accepted Christ into her heart. She was nine at the time. In her teenage years she taught the little ones about Jesus in Sunday school and Bible school.

My greatest and most fulfilling times, as a parent, were having my family in church and doing God's work. I feel there was nothing we could have done differently, in any circumstance, to change the things we were to endure in the coming years.

In 1980 Janelle's husband strangled our lovely daughter to death. I remember how distraught and heartbroken I was when I heard the local news report. How I thanked God and praised Him for having laid the burden on my heart, as a parent, to take my children to church. I knew at that moment Janelle was with the Lord.

At the gravesite I told the Lord, "I don't like what has happened but I will accept it and be thankful for the time we had her with us." We enjoyed her so much.

People tell us, "Time will take care of the hurt." But the emptiness and hurt just goes on and on.

In 1981 I sat through a murder trial, which was so trying, with my son Jeffrey by my side. Yet, again the Lord was so close. I felt as though a protective dome covered us. As the verdict was soon to be given, a calm assurance came from the Lord that all would be right. And it was. Justice prevailed.

We may never know what trials there will be to conquer as we go through life, but God doesn't tell us of all the joys we might experience either. He does tell us we will have joy unspeakable and full of glory. If we just hang on, the joy will come in the morning. *Psalms 30:5b: Weeping may endure for a night, But joy comes in the morning. (NKJV)*

1 Thessalonians 5:18: *In everything give thanks for this is the will of God in Christ Jesus concerning you. (KJV)* It was difficult to thank God at times, but I always did and to this day I still do for giving us our three children. I also thank Him for the time I had with the two we lost.

Many nights I sat in darkness, praying God would let the night end because I couldn't handle any more. The next night I would sit in darkness and pray God would not let morning come because I couldn't handle another day. He carried me each night and day. Soon I found His arms were so much longer than ours. He reaches down for us and carries us to a brighter day.

Each loss I have experienced has felt like a slice of my heart being cut away until very little remained. I realized I could not fill it with anger, bitterness, fear and doubt. I never questioned God nor will I in the future. That would be wasted time I could use to praise Him for the precious memories we have.

It took much time and many prayers to reach the point where I could say that the good and happy memories overrode the bad ones.

I cannot imagine trying to get through any trial in life without God. He is always there for us regardless of the size of the problem.

I am grateful for a loving and supportive family who carried me through with intercessory prayers. There were times I didn't know what to pray but realized God knew my heart and knew it was broken. He understood my pain and grief. When I could be very still and listen, soon I could pray again.

Today as a hurting parent being healed by God's

power, I reach out to other parents, who are grieving over the loss of a child. May I encourage you with praise and thanksgiving to our God, from a mother, who has had her heart broken. I share and understand your pain. Trust in God. He will carry you through.

Cecelia Trivitt spent her life in Southwest Missouri and lives presently in Springfield with her son, Jeff. Born in a Christian home, she appreciates her heritage. She accepted the Lord at an early age and continues to serve Him. She experiences His presence through the valleys and the mountaintops. Cecelia ministers in Sunday school, Bible school, Bible study, churches, nursing homes and to other groups in sermons and songs. She loves speaking and entertaining elderly people.

Charlotte's Comments

This mother lost two children, one only ten days old. What heartbreak she encountered and still she praised the Lord. Later in life she endured the loss of yet another child. She continued to put her faith and trust in Him.

What a terrible thing it must be to have a child murdered by someone, especially someone they loved and trusted. Yet, it happens everyday. Each person murdered belongs to a parent. What a test of faith those parents must experience. Not only do they grieve the death of their child, but they must either forgive, or not, the person who took their child's life.

As Christians, we know we must forgive in order to receive the answers to our prayers. Scripture is pretty clear. Even in the Lord's Prayer, our Savior says, "Forgive us our debts as we forgive our debtors." So with the same measure we forgive, we are forgiven. I want to be forgiven and have my prayers answered, so I have learned to forgive.

In our own strength we may not be able to forgive in these situations, but with the help of our God we can. I sometimes have to start by saying, "God I can't forgive. I'm not yet even willing, so help me be willing to be willing to forgive and continue to work in my heart until I can forgive." He has answered every time.

Cecelia's strong faith helped her endure and brought her through this terrible tragedy to a place of joy. Only God can do this!

Prayer: *Lord, help us to forgive that we might be forgiven. Help us to be willing to be willing. Bless those parents who have lost their child at the hands of someone else. May they be able to forgive. Help the one who took their child's life find You and Your forgiving love. In Jesus Name. Amen.*

194

Chapter Twenty
Death and His Special Grace
By Jackie Richardson

I had been 'scrubbed' for a little over two hours assisting the surgeon on a case in the operating room. Sarah, my secretary came into the room and said, "The boss wants to see you in her office as soon as possible."

"It'll be a little while because I need to finish this case," I said.

Sarah came back into the room several times to tell me Nancy, the nursing administrator had called me again and it was very important.

"I'm supposed to take you to the office," she said.

My first thought was Sarah's mother had passed away and Nancy knew I would be some support to her.

When the case finally finished I went to Nancy's office. Nancy and I had developed a close friendship. Mostly because of the common bond we shared as Christian nurses. She was a remarkable woman and nurse. When I walked into the office, I knew something was wrong but I still thought it concerned Sarah.

Nancy began by telling me they had found our

son, Phil's, body.

"Is he okay?" It was a stupid question for a nurse to ask, but I asked it anyway.

Nancy looked at me with tears in her eyes, "No, Jackie, he's dead." She added that my husband, Mike, was at another hospital identifying the body. She called my daughters and my pastors to come be with me until Mike arrived.

I went numb. *It can't be true. This can't be happening to us.*

After Mike arrived our pastors accompanied us home. Within a couple of hours, our pastors brought us to reality and helped us realize we needed to start preparing for a funeral. We were at a loss as to what to do next. Our pastors were friends of a man that worked at a funeral home nearby. They called him. After a few minutes they said, "We'll go with you and help make the arrangements."

We realized Phil was not covered by any insurance policy. We had to drop him from the family policy because of his age. He was married but had no insurance coverage, due to the expense.

The man at the funeral home helped guide us through the process; showing us patience and kindness the entire time. After the first few things were discussed, he took us to the back so we could select a coffin. The word coffin still sounds cold and painful to me. I knew as we started to look, we needed to look at the least expensive they had to offer. It was not what I wanted but I knew we had to. It felt like my heart just kept breaking apart.

Since there was no insurance coverage, our pastor and his friend suggested we announce in the paper, "In lieu of flowers, monies will be accepted to cover funeral expenses." I despised the thought but knew we needed the help.

Funeral arrangements completed, we returned home to our other children. Our daughter-in-law came to the house with their children.

The next morning I looked at the newspaper, which read, "Young Man Commits Suicide at Conroe."

I yelled at God saying, "I can not accept this and the fact our son might be in hell." I am not an emotional person but I reacted that day as emotional as anyone could have. My pain with the death of Phil was enough but this headline on top of that was more than I could handle.

For several weeks I was angry at God and

continued to questions His faithfulness to me. At one point I actually told God He lied and His Word was not true. I heard a whisper of a voice speak to me.

"Do you believe it because it is My Word or do you have to see it to believe it?"

I quickly asked God to forgive me and told Him I did trust Him and His precious Word.

With the help and generosity of our friends at work, our church and our families, we collected enough money to cover the funeral expenses and enough to purchase a marker for the gravesite. We knew God blessed us through these wonderful people. I no longer could question his faithfulness.

My husband and I held each other close as the days went by. We received a call from our family in Missouri. My mother-in-law had passed away. We quickly notified our daughters and made arrangements to drive from Texas to Missouri for her funeral. It seemed like death continued to surround us. We unexpectedly lost my husband's brother and three days later lost my mother. A few months following, my oldest sister passed away.

But it was the loss of our son that seemed to grip us in the pain of hurt that I cannot explain. The loss of a child is just something a parent should not have to go through.

We began to question what we could have possibly done differently or what we should not have done. We discovered studies, which proved that the majority of couples to lose a child under these conditions ended up separating. We thank God for His grace, which gave us strength to make it through together.

On one of our trips to Missouri we stopped at a Baptist Book Store and I found the most beautiful song. It became my song and my testimony. The song is titled "A Very Special Grace." The words ministered to my heart and soul. As I sang it, God used its message to help me heal. He also used it to minister to others when they heard it. I sang it for a couple of funerals and in many church services in Texas, Missouri and California. I sang it at my place of work. Each time it ministered to me and to others.

God continued to help us heal and He ministered to our family during the worse time of our life.

I must share with you that when my brother-in-law passed away God did a wonderful thing for us coming home from his funeral. I drifted off to sleep and in a dream I saw Phil reach out his hand and say, "Come on home, Grandma."

I shared this with my husband but not with the rest of family. My sister called three days later to tell of my mother's death. She called me again that same day and asked me if I thought God ever sent someone's spirit back to earth.

"If He feels it is necessary, yes, He will." I said.

She then told me she thought mother had already died but all of a sudden mother reached out her hand and said, "Oh, honey."

"I felt like mother had seen Phil," she said,

My heart did rejoice within me as I thought, *Thank you, Lord, for letting me know Phil and my mother are both safely home.*

I still miss Phil but I know he is in a better place and he is waiting for my husband and me to join him.

At the time of Phil's death I thought, *Oh, God, any way but this. A car wreck, murdered, but not this way, not from suicide.*

I have since realized that it doesn't matter how you lose a child, it hurts beyond what any words can express. But I do know God and His wonderful grace are sufficient to see you through the valley of the shadow of death. Yes, His grace is sufficient. *And He said to me,*

200

"My grace is sufficient for you, for My strength is made perfect in weakness." Therefore most gladly I will rather boast in my infirmities, that the power of Christ may rest upon me. 2 Corinthians 12:9 (NKJV)

MY SON
By Jackie Richardson

The tears no longer come. Yet, the pain still lingers on.
Only God can understand how much I miss my son.
Gone from this life all too soon,
leaving such sorrow behind.
A precious gift God loaned me for a few years.
Then he left and my eyes filled with many tears.
Memories so sweet still linger on,
even though he now is gone.
His smile, which could win anyone with its charm,
forever stays in my mind and lingers on.
His head on my shoulder will no longer be,
only memories, but no longer his face I will see.
The pain and struggle his life on this earth brought,
still leaves my heart and mind with many thoughts.
I think of his days as a child and then as a teen
and all of the days in between.
The dreams we shared which never came to pass,
because he left this life all too fast.
I know you're at rest now, my son.
Your winning smile still lingers on.
The love we shared as a family,
Brings comfort to your father and me.
I will never stop missing you but I know it's true;
someday we will meet again beyond the blue.

Written in memory of my loving son who died

201

from an overdose. I still miss you so much, my dear Phil.
I still remember how you and Faith would put your
heads on my shoulder and look up at me with those big
brown eyes and say, "Please Mom."

Having your son, Shannon, live with us reminds
us so much of you. He does not take your place because
no one ever could. He has independently won his place
in our hearts. He is his own unique, individual person.
He is intelligent and has a great potential to accomplish
remarkable things in this life – if he will just do it.

I'm looking forward to seeing you again when I
reach Heaven. I know you, along with my mother and
my oldest sister, are all waiting for me.

*Jackie Richardson is a nurse manager, motivational
speaker and writer. Born in Cape Girardeau, MO. She
received her nursing degree at Southeast Missouri
University. Active in church activities for the past 55
years, she devotes much time to teaching others within
the church and her work area. She served for 18 years
on the Houston Community College Surgical Technology
program by teaching and on the admission and advisory
boards and received special recognition for her
contributions. Her main goal in life is to be a vessel of
honor for the Lord.*

Charlotte's Comments

One of the worst fears a parent ever faces might
be whether or not their child made it to heaven. Jackie

rejoiced when God gave her this assurance. My own son wasted his life on drugs and alcohol, but I chose to believe he knew the Savior. He accepted Jesus as a young boy and then turned back to Him in prison another time. Drugs and alcohol held my son bound, and he found it difficult to serve Him. I pray he made peace with Him before he left this earth.

We can't judge another man's heart or whether or not someone has a relationship with the Lord. We cannot know whether our loved one believed that Christ died, was buried, and rose again according to the Scripture, so that person can be saved, unless they tell us. The grace of God and the blood of Christ saves us all. It is not something we earn but remains a free gift. Even if we think we know by their behavior, who can be sure?

Even if you aren't sure whether or not your child knew Christ, God can give you peace. No one can know another's heart, except God. Again, we have to leave it with Him and trust Him in our grief.

Prayer: *Lord, I pray for those parents who are not sure if their child knew You. I pray You will give them peace and assurance that You have it all in hand. If their child knew You, I pray they will somehow find that assurance.*

If not, I pray You will comfort them and let them know they themselves can know You. Somehow You will work it all out - for there will be no tears in heaven. In Jesus Name. Amen.

Chapter Twenty-One
Loss of Joy
By Charlotte Holt

After experiencing pain in my arms for two months, I finally sought out my cardiologist advice. On June 31, he directed me to the emergency room. He discovered three blocked arteries and my discomfort proved to be angina. Two of the blood vessels to my aorta were ninety to ninety-nine percent blocked and another one thirty. On July 5, I underwent a triple heart by-pass. I returned to work in October after three months of recuperation, just as the holiday season began gearing up. It felt good to be back among the living.

By November, I was used to working again. My routine returned to normal and I felt confident with my workload. I arrived home one afternoon, not suspecting anything different, however, a foreboding in my spirit for several days prompted me to pray. No sooner did I enter the door of my home than my husband met me with the statement: "I have some bad news for you."

My world began to spin and come apart. *What's wrong? Who's sick? Has there been an accident?* All these questions surged through my mind. I'm almost sure I voiced some of them.

"Honey, I'm sorry, but John was killed in a car accident. I'm so sorry," he sobbed.

My first reaction was one of denial, which most people say they experience. "No, no, tell me it's not true. It can't be. Not my John!" I sobbed. Anger towards my husband for telling me such a thing flooded over me. I certainly didn't want to believe it.

My husband took me into his arms to comfort me. He held me as I cried out over and over in anguish, repeating my denial. I then went into a numbing shock. I could not feel or think of anything except how bad I hurt. I could not believe my precious son, who for many years had been my joy, could be gone.

The past few years had been hard. John rebelled and got involved in drugs through the influence of his older brother, Louis.

A year earlier, John was hospitalized and lay in a comatose state following a motorcycle accident, which resulted in brain surgery. We thought at the time he might not recover. But through the prayers of the saints, he survived. He went through a period of adjustment after surgery. The removal of a portion of his temporal lobe affected his short-term memory. Still, he made progress and inched his way back to being the John I knew as my joy. Our relationship, too, was on the mend, but his life was still a mess.

John needed to appear in court for payment of back rent on an apartment where he once lived. I don't know all of the details. He now lived with a former teacher. He told me he intended to marry her at one point, but never informed me he did. Maybe, he didn't want to because of my disapproval, or perhaps he forgot due to the short-term memory loss from the brain surgery. He substituted in the school where she taught and loved it, which seemed to be a highlight of his life at the time.

The thing he enjoyed most was driving his Corvette. As a youngster, he loved Corvettes and said he would someday own one. So, when he received a settlement from the motorcycle wreck, he bought his dream car. He shined that blue with white racing stripped 1987 automobile and took great pride in it. He liked to take it out onto a gravel road, in Arizona where he lived, and drive it very fast. On this particular day, he rolled the vehicle, pinning himself against the steering wheel. The impact crushed his chest. On the way to the hospital in the ambulance he drew his last breath.

The days after his death passed in a fog, but somehow with the prayers of friends and loved ones, I made it through. John's wife, Grace, had no money to speak of and no insurance for his burial. Thankfully, Charles and I kept an insurance policy on him, which I started around his tenth birthday. He turned twenty-two a few months earlier. God saw the road ahead, even though we could not.

We arranged John's travel to return his body to my childhood hometown for the service and burial. The funeral director knew my family and agreed to perform the services. We buried John in the family cemetery, not far from my Mom and Dad.

When I look back, I see the many ways God provided for me: the plots reserved for our family, the insurance we did not allow to lapse, and my family and long time friends supported me by bringing food and tending to whatever else needed to be done. The pastor who performed the funeral was a friend I once dated in high school. God had everything covered for me, even the void in my heart. He filled it with His love.

One slight problem remained. I had no idea how to locate my older son, Louis. After trying to reach him at his last place of residence, I finally gave his location to the Lord. "Lord, only You know Louis's whereabouts and if You want him at the funeral, You bring him there." I prayed.

John died on November 19, the week of Thanksgiving. When making the funeral arrangements, I called John's father, his grandmother, and the rest of the family. The day before the funeral Louis contacted his grandmother, who lived about 100 miles from my hometown. Passing through her city, he called and wanted to know if he and some friends could come to her house for Thanksgiving. She informed him of John's death. He and his friends drove to my brother's house, where we were staying. God came through again. Louis showed up in time for the funeral.

Many other circumstances during the funeral and the days ahead showcased God's handiwork. I realized, even in the midst of my hurt and pain, He had everything in control. I rested in the hope we have in Him, a hope only those who know Him can have. He kept me strong in my weakness. *And he said unto me, My grace is sufficient for thee: for my strength is made perfect in weakness. Most gladly therefore will I rather glory in my infirmities, that the power of Christ may rest upon me.* 2 Corinthians 12:9 (KJV)

Yes, I cried buckets of tears. The doctor put me on some sleep medication, something I would not recommend, for it proved to be somewhat addictive. I struggled to get off it. But with God's help again, I broke free.

The days and months following the funeral proved difficult, but God showed up strong. He held me up, strengthened, encouraged me, and helped me through it all.

At times I questioned why, but I knew about God's sovereignty. He knew best. Perhaps, John would have turned away from Him. During the time before his death he tried to follow Him, and I felt he made peace with Him. Some months before he died, we talked about his salvation. I think it made him get down and do business with God and ask for His forgiveness. All we have to do is ask forgiveness and really mean it, if we stray from Him. He is a God of second chances, over and over.

I found times of being angry with John for dying. I forgave him for leaving me. I forgave him for driving too fast. I went through times of blaming myself. I wondered what I did wrong to make him take the rebellious route and use drugs. I questioned if I drove him away to such a different life than I wanted for him.

I forgave myself. If we don't forgive ourselves, we are saying we are greater than God, because He forgives us. I finally realized it was not my fault, and each person makes his or her own choices. No, I don't think John chose to die, but he lived a lifestyle, which led to an early death for him. I forgave him for his choices.

One thing I learned during this time is that God looks at death differently than we do. To Him, death marks the beginning of a new life for those who believe – a beginning of eternal life for those who love and trust Him. We look at death as the end, but God sees it as the beginning of eternity.

If we look at death His way, we can have confidence we will see our loved ones again. This gives us the blessed hope we read about in 1 Peter 1:4: *to an inheritance incorruptible and undefiled and that does not fade away, reserved in heaven for you.*

I have gone through different phases of the grieving process. The denial, anger and acceptance stages are behind me, but I will never quit missing John. I especially miss him during holidays and birthdays. Some days I think of him for no reason at all. Other times something reminds me of him. God comforts me in the midst of it. That blessed hope continues to remind me I will see him again and next time it will be forever.

At times I feel the loss more acutely than others, but God strengthens me in the process. He uses me to help others through their grief. He has shown me how to trust Him in my grief. He can comfort other's hearts as He has mine.

Each time I think of my son now, it is with appreciation for the time I spent with him. I remember the good times we shared. I now can be thankful for those times. I don't dwell on the hurt and pain of my loss. I have moved on with my life and enjoy each day God gives me. I have learned to trust Him with every part of my life, perhaps, because of this most difficult trial.

God has given me more than I could ever dare hope, think or dream. He strengthened me through the loss I experienced in my life. I thank Him for the love of those around me: my husband, my stepchildren, grandchildren, friends, family and my brothers and sisters in Christ. Suffering this loss gave me a new appreciation of those things I have gained.

I pray those reading this book can do the same

with their grief. I know God can turn it into good just as He did for me.

I encourage them to share their story with those who are grieving, show them how they came through, encourage them and help them know they can make it too, listen to them and love them with the love of the One, who they can trust in their grief.

After John's death I wrote this:

Ode To A Son
By Charlotte Holt

When we've raised a child, and he gets to be a teen.
He doesn't know if he's fish, fowl or in between.
Only yesterday he was just a tiny boy.
He sat on his mother's lap and played with a toy.

How the time flies, and we wonder where it's gone.
We sit up late, wait for him, or his call on the phone.
We keep him in our thoughts when he's out at night.
Is he doing wrong or right?

If only we could make the choice of what he'd do.
No one else can live his life, not even you!
In our thoughts, our mind, and heart each day.
He's the first on our list when we pray.

How we'd like to shield him from the world and sin.
How we long to talk with him again.
He'd rather listen to his friend's advise of what to do.
His peers are more important now than you.

It hurts to see him break away from his boyhood home.

Trusting Him In Your Grief/Charlotte Holt

It's hard to see him go other places to roam.
He ventures into the world to try his wings.
We wish we could tell him so many things.

Some sons make us happy and some make us sad.
Some end up being good, and some go bad.
We hope and pray our son will never go astray.
Sometimes it happens the other way.

A call in the middle of the night, "Who could it be?"
You look at the clock, a quarter past three.
A voice says, "Are you the parent of this young man?"
You reply, "Yes sir, I am."

"Do you know where your son is?"
"Yes, sir, he's sleeping in his bed."
"Better take another look." Our heart fills with dread."
Visions flash through our mind. *Is he alive or dead?*

"No, sir, he's down here in jail.
Would you like to come and pay his bail?"
Our heart race; Now we're awake and on our feet.
What has happened to our son, this one so sweet?

Tears fill our eyes and a prayer crosses our tongue,
We rush to see if we can bring him home.
Although we may be angry, we're glad he's alive.
We pray both we, and he, will survive.

"What have I done wrong? What is my sin?
Haven't I taught him right again and again?"
We drop to our knees and take time to pray.
"Oh, dear Lord, help me through this day."

A peace envelops us, and we know God's there.
Even in the midst of our despair.

We bring him home and hope things improve with love.
We endeavor to show him ours and the Father's above.

Each day we pray he will change.
His life he will rearrange.
A change comes over him like a flood.
When he becomes washed in Jesus blood.

He no longer brings us grief.
We both find great relief.
A Son of God, he's alive and not dead.
A new path he starts to tread.

We thank our Father above.
He has given us a brand new son to love.
We know in this fabulous hour.
Our son's life was changed by God's great power.

Charlotte Holt *retired from 30 years of teaching,
authored* Praise The Lord for Roaches! And Anything
Else That Bugs You. The Texas State Inspirational
Writers Alive! elected her 'Writer of the Year' in
2002. *Her articles and poems appear online, in
anthologies and magazines. She deposited two sons in
Heaven but enjoys three stepchildren and three step
grandchildren. Her greatest accomplishments entail
knowing the Lord and being married for 32 years to
Charles Holt, owner of North Houston Exterminators.
They reside in Kingwood, Texas.*

Charlotte's Comments

If this has happened in your child's life, if he has
made a choice for God, then you know, you will see him
again. The surrender and choice may, or may not, be this

dramatic but you have a hope. This choice can be at the last moment of his life or one he made years ago. If he did not make this choice, you can still be assured God will take care of you, heal your heart, and give you a new song to sing for His love toward you. *Psalms 30:5: For His anger is but for a moment, His favor is for a lifetime; Weeping may last for the night, But a shout of joy {comes} in the morning. (NASB)*

Prayer: *Lord, I thank You for healing our hearts and giving us a new song to sing because of Your love toward us. I pray we will come to know and understand the depth, height, width and magnitude of that love. For Your love is stronger, deeper, higher, wider, and better than anything the world has to give. In Jesus Name. Amen.*

Chapter Twenty-Two
The Promise Of The Rainbow
By Sylvia Woody

It caught my eye when I first entered Dee Gee's, a unique gift shop on the Atlantic Beach strand. It was just what I was looking for. The music box was even more perfect when I heard the tinkling notes of "Somewhere Over the Rainbow." It would be the ideal gift for this six-year-old girl that I had in mind. Little did I know at the time this was foreshadowing an event, which would forever change and confirm the promise of the rainbow.

On my way back to the beach cottage, I unwrapped the little music box and turned the key. As the familiar melody about the rainbow filled the air, I hummed along, reflecting back to younger years. The rainbow had always given me a sense of awe and wonder...

Growing up on a farm, the wide-open spaces offered a perfect setting for viewing a rainbow. When one appeared after a spring rain, I would rush to find an even better view in an attempt to capture the beauty of the fleeting spectrum of colors. Even then there were thoughts that perhaps there is more than the age-old legend of a "pot of gold" at the end of a rainbow.

In my late teens, the rainbow became more significant because of a family crisis. It happened when my two older sisters and I were attending the same college. We received news that our father had died suddenly from a heart attack. His premature death devastated all of us. My older brother, who attended another college, joined us with my mother, and two younger sisters at home for the funeral.

Our hearts were heavy as we sat together in the small rural church on that crisp, clear February day. We were especially sad because our father was not a professed Christian.

After the services, and during the silent drive back to our home, my brother finally broke the heaviness with a well-intended word of consolation. The words were barely out when we saw it. Above the barn amidst the fleecy clouds appeared a most perfect rainbow. We stared at its radiant beauty.

"Isn't there a Scripture about a rainbow in the Bible?" my sister asked.

We went to the den and pulled the family Bible from the bookcase as soon as we arrived home. Ruth quickly turned through the first pages while the rest of us looked on. She had no trouble finding the scripture. The verse in Genesis 9:13 was distinctly underlined. This was unique because it was the only marked passage in the Bible. We looked at each other in disbelief! Was this a sign from God?

"I prayed for a sign," Mother said.

The peace that followed assured us, especially Mother, that our father was, indeed, with his heavenly Father.

The years passed, and through trials and crises, the God of my youth became a more personal God. My commitment to Him deepened and became an important part of my life.

The blessing of a husband and three beautiful children granted me the fulfillment that every woman dreams of. My husband and I met while he was stationed at a military base near the college I attended. We were married and I lived the next 20 years as a military wife and mother. After my husband's retirement from the Marine Corps, we moved to Waco where he obtained his law degree at Baylor. Afterwards, we moved to Victoria where he set up his law practice.

The years passed and the expectation of

happiness for my daughter, Joanie, and sons, Kelly and Tom, became a focus in my life. My relationship to Joanie remained close even after she graduated from college and moved to Fort Worth to work for the Kenneth Copeland Ministry.

Joanie's heart's desire was to marry. In 1989, at 32 years of age, she met and soon married a fine young Christian man. They came from similar backgrounds. Both worked for Christian ministries. I was so happy for Joan and looked forward to a fulfilling life for the two of them, and hopefully some grandchildren to spoil.

It was the summer of 1990 at Atlantic Beach that I last saw Joan. She and her husband flew in from Texas to join us for a family reunion and to meet the rest of my family. I arrived there early to spend time with other family members. We had three wonderful days together. Just before leaving to meet the plane, Joanie reached out and hugged me and said she loved me and added she'd see me in Texas very soon.

The day before I planned to fly back to Victoria from North Carolina, I was at Mother's house packing when my husband, Larry, called me with the news that Joanie had been killed in a car accident. He was in his office when he received the call from Fort Worth. It was

Joanie's first day back at work. Drizzling rain made the roads slippery. She might have been speeding, hit a slick spot, causing her to lose control of her car. The car hydroplaned and hit a telephone pole. She died instantly.

Our oldest son was in California at the time and our youngest at Texas A&M, in College Station. I flew back to Victoria that same day. My husband and I picked up Kelly from the airport and Tom drove in from college. The next day we drove to Fort Worth for the funeral. Joan's husband had made all the arrangements.

The service was held at Lake Country Baptist Church outside of Fort Worth. This funeral, however, was unlike my father's of many years ago. People packed the church and there was an air of joyous celebration of my daughter's life and the sureness of her eternity with her Savior. The words spoken forth were comforting and encouraging to each family member.

Earlier in the day, intermittent rains prevailed; but as condolences and regrets were extended at the graveside services, the sun came out and the clouds soon dissipated. My sisters, nieces, and nephews flew in for the funeral and were so supportive that it made it especially difficult to say goodbye to them as they drove to the airport. Mother, unfortunately, was unable to come but I found out later she was praying constantly back in North Carolina.

Later, that same evening, Sue, one of my sisters, called and excitedly related the events of their trip. She said that after they boarded the plane, they settled down for the solemn flight back home. Talking quietly, they tried to make sense out of tragic circumstances. They had been airborne less than an hour when Sue looked out the window and saw stretched across the sky, a rainbow, in all of its brilliant colors. My niece, sitting across the aisle, exclaimed, "There's another rainbow on this side!"

They all stood up, and searching the sky they saw not two, but six!

Sue's account of the details reinforced my feeling that again God revealed Himself through the rainbow.

Heaven is over and beyond the rainbow. The magnificent arc of colors is just a tiny glimmer of the resplendence of heaven itself. It is God's radiant energy visibly expressed through a series of vibrant colors. God created the rainbow as a form of communication to show His loving promises, His pledge to us, and His Covenant with us. It is a sign from Him that our sufferings will soon fade.

In the months following Joan's death, I felt God's presence and His comfort in a way I did not know were possible. It seemed incredible how He had been preparing my heart all these years to face this tragic crisis in my life. His divine strength allowed me to minister healing to my husband and Joan's husband. In retrospect, it was God's mercy and grace to me.

Sylvia Woody, 67, homemaker, wife and mother of two sons, with three grandchildren.
Her interest and hobbies include writing, reading, traveling and scrap booking.
She teaches Sunday school and a weekly Bible study, does missionary work in Mexico and speaks at women's meetings. Sylvia has been published in *Angels On Earth" and Golden Words publications. She resides in Victoria, Texas, with her husband, Larry, USMC Major and attorney, both retired. They have traveled extensively in Europe.

Charlotte's Comments

What an awesome God we serve. He gave us the rainbow as a promise of better things to come. He gave this mother the rainbow as a special sign throughout her life to prepare her for the most painful time ever. Each time He gave her this sign it showed her there were better things to come. Someday, she will experience the greatest blessing of all, when she sees her loved ones face-to-face and lives with them forever.

We all have this waiting for us if we have trusted Him. Trust Him for He will keep His promise.

Prayer: *Lord, we thank You that Your promises are yea and amen. We thank You for being faithful to do what You say You will. Unlike most other men, there is no variableness of turning with You. Your Word is forever settled and true. Thank You for the rainbow that reminds us of Your promises. Help us to know, that like Noah and his family, there are better days ahead for us just like there will be for Sylvia. In Jesus Name. Amen.*

Chapter Twenty-Three
My Grief and My Deliverance
By Darlene Patton Stelljes

Friday, September 1996, a day I will always remember. I took my son, Dwayne, to a neurologist after he experienced a seizure while barbequing in his backyard on Labor Day. He walked to the waiting room and motioned me to come back into the doctor's office, where he underwent examination. The doctor joined us in the hall and said, "I think your son has a brain tumor." Just like that. Like it was no big deal. I could not fathom, at that moment, what the next four months would hold. Every emotion imaginable flowed through my body.

On September 23, one week after his first brain surgery we celebrated his thirty-second birthday. He had been diagnosed with melanoma, the deadliest type of skin cancer. The brain tumors stemmed from a mole removed from his back seven years earlier. Even though they ruled the tissue around the mole as being clean, no spreading, it evidently entered his blood stream, which he never knew until the day in the doctor's office. The last place tumors form is in the brain. This was the situation in September 1996.

Prayer! No one has ever prayed more fervently than our family and church friends. Confident of God, we prayed. I believed God would heal my only child. I read in Genesis of Abraham offering his only son, Isaac, as a sacrifice. I cried and found comfort when God stopped Abraham from killing him. Confident God would do the same for me, I released Dwayne and felt God would heal him.

I thought of Mary, the Mother of Jesus, and the grief she endured. When Simeon told her, "a sword will pierce through your soul," how could she have known what the days ahead would hold?

My son left this life on January 6, 1997. I felt that sword and sometimes it stayed for a while. I understood how utterly helpless Mary must have felt as she stood by and watched her son die, able only to love and hurt for her young man as she knelt and wept.

Our family has known its share of sorrow. My sister's fifteen-year-old daughter was killed in a car accident, and my brother's daughter was murdered at the age of nineteen. We lost my father in 1994. He was a minister for over fifty-five years. Many times I heard Dad say, "you can take those trials and either grow bitter or better. You make the choice."

The days passed. I knew hundreds of people were praying for me. I could not. I felt numb.

"He will live forever in your memory," some said.

LIVE! That's exactly what he won't do. I wanted to scream. *Blessed [are] they that mourn: for they shall be comforted.* Matthew 5:4 (NKJV)

That passage of Scripture is different when things happen to you. When I mourned the least, I remembered my son the best.

Dwayne was a smiling, charming young man. He was my friend. We had a special relationship. He fathered two beautiful little girls. Why was he taken so young? We all needed him. When he died – a part of me was gone. For months I laid questions before God and received no answers. It may not have been a locked door, but the silence was just as difficult to endure.

Grief is like fear, the same fluttering in the stomach, the same restlessness. You find it hard to take in what anyone says, or maybe it's just uninteresting. You don't only suffer, but keep thinking about the fact that you suffer. Grief is not a trip you can pack for. It can be utterly lonely, even when you have those who love you around.

All through this God stayed with me. He carried me. He loved me when I was unlovable. I really think His heart broke for me. One night close to Mother's Day the year after Dwayne died, I cried from the depths of my soul. I stood in my closet because I didn't want my husband to hear me.

"God, where are you?" Just as soon as I said it, a voice came to me.

"I KNOW WHERE YOU ARE."

I knew this was a heavenly reassurance. A sense of peace came over me and I immediately recognized His love and care. I knew He knew my grief. I did not experience an overnight release but received a slow healing. I realized I must make a conscious decision to get past my grief and go on with life. I knew Dwayne would want me to make this choice as well. No, the pain didn't completely go away, but God helped me to learn how to live with it. Today I am glad I made the choice to grow better.

I have had several very vivid dreams and experiences that gave me a warm feeling. I learned to lean on Jesus and feel the wonder of His love. Today, I live with the promise that I will see my son again.

Inscribed on my son's memorial: *weeping may*

endure for a night, but joy cometh in the morning. Psalm 30:5 (KJV)

Oh, what a blessed assurance.

That Smile
In Honor Of My Son, Dwayne Marshburn
By Darlene Patton Stelljes

Years ago at the age of almost eighteen,
I gave birth to a baby boy – the prettiest little baby I'd
ever seen.
He won my heart immediately when his tiny fingers
gripped mine.
He squinted at the light and I was on cloud nine.
It was then that I saw it for the first time – that smile.

When he was just barely walking, he came into the
house happily talking.
Something was in his arms and he looked at me with
great charm.
And said, "Pease, Mommy, Pease can I keep it?"
A small stray kitten he gently held - he was already
smitten I could tell.
How could I resist when he looked up at me with – that
smile.

Then I put him in day care school, as I went to work, I
felt so cruel.
At work I could hardly see, for the tears filled my eyes.
I just knew I could hear his muffled cries.
So off I went, rushing to get back to my baby,
Running inside, I saw him sitting on the lap of the day
care lady.
He looked up at me with big bright eyes and there it was
– that smile.

Then there was the time when he was about nine.
He had gained weight, as heaviness is a Patton trait,
He came home so sad and nothing would help get him
glad.
A teacher at school had made fun of him, where the kids
were playing in the gym,
Then through his tears at a book he did look, there he
saw a picture of a baby wallaby,
Laughing, he exclaimed, "Oh, Mom, look this kangaroo
is fatter than me."
There again it was – that smile.

Into his teens he went, the little boy look was gone,
Tall and thin – so handsome he had grown,
A charming personality, a beautiful head of hair,
Wherever we went you could see the girls stare.
In return he would look, with a twinkle in his eye.
And there it was – that smile.

All through his life, whenever he felt I needed help,
He would be there for me, saying sweet things and
helping me through,
Saying, "Mom, remember I wouldn't be here if it wasn't
for you."
Then, of course, I would have to laugh, and the bad
feelings would pass.
For how could I stay sad, when all I needed to see was –
that smile.

In his last months, even through all of his pain and fear,
Most all the time, he would be so positive and full of
great cheer,
As he expressed his thankfulness to God for all his
family and friends,
Whenever anyone would come to see him,
He would always have – that smile.

Eight and one-half months ago today, he went into rest.
And there are so many things about him that I miss.
For we had a oneness that's hard to describe.
As I stand here before you today, I can say with great pride,
"Dwayne was a wonderful son and a part of me is gone.
I can only hope I will see him in that Heavenly home.
For there I once again want to see – that smile."

Darlene Patton Stelljes, born in Ft. Worth, Texas to Clyde & Otella Patton, moved to Houston at three months old for her father to Pastor a church, loves to sing gospel music. She resides in Spring, Texas. Her husband of over 30 years, Fritz Stelljes, passed away after a long illness which she was his caretaker. She deposited one child in heaven, has two granddaughters, and four great-grandchildren. She shares the love of her husband's four children, in-laws and two grandchildren. She worked for the same oil industry-consulting firm for over 30 years, but is now retired. She attends the Gospel Assembly Church in Humble, Texas.

Charlotte's Comments

Yes, we can grow bitter or better. Our choices depend on us, and our trust in God. Even those of us, who know the Lord and have known Him for a long time, fail to trust Him to the fullest extent with portions of our life, or people in our life. Every day we must chose Him and His Word. As Joshua said, "Chose you this day whom you will serve."

When one loses a child, it is sometimes hard to

release them to God or trust Him in this horrific tragedy. Many often think, *God could have prevented this.* They then hold God responsible for their loss and grow angry with Him. Some never get over it. I pray if you are one of those, who want to hold God responsible, you will realize, God is sovereign and you need to get over it.

He knows what's best and He looks at death differently than we do. Death is the beginning of eternity for the child of God. Death is inevitable for all of us. We will all die. Yes, it is generally unnatural for us to bury our children, but it happens everyday. Remember in this world we will have tribulations, but He tells us to be of good cheer for He has overcome the world.

When we lose someone we love, if we chose life instead of death for ourselves, figuratively, God will bring new life into us and see us through in peace and joy, literally. We may have to work for our peace by the choices we make, but He will give it to us.

Prayer: *Lord, help us to get over any bitterness or pain associated with our child's death. Help us to chose life and live again in fullness of joy by walking in Your way and by Your Spirit. Thank You for the peace and joy You bring into our life. I ask You to fill us all with these fruits of the Spirit along with all the other benefits You have* *for us. Help us to overcome, be of good cheer, and live beyond ourselves in You. In Jesus Name. Amen.*

Chapter Twenty-Four
No Easier the Second Time Around
By Charlotte Holt

After the death of my son, John, his brother Louis turned his life around for a time. He stayed in Oklahoma, where we buried his brother, found a job, went back to church and tried to get his life in order. He made a new commitment to the Lord.

Louis accepted Christ at a young age but drifted off into the drug and alcohol world when he entered his teens. He spent a good deal of his life following rock groups around the country, selling drugs to get by. He plunged in and out of jail, and even went to prison, for selling and distributing drugs. He kept me on my knees for many years.

Louis's renewed commitment gave me hope that he would turn his life around and go in a different direction. For a time, he did. He went back to school and almost got his certification in graphic arts. Just before he accomplished this, he started using drugs again and the school officials kicked him out. Our hearts broke. Charles and I helped and sacrificed in order to get him through school.

After a time of further drug involvement and running from the law, he settled down in Waco, Texas, not far from where we lived. He took up residence with a lady he knew from his past. In some ways she helped settle him, and he started working for a top publisher in their print shop.

Louis and his lady friend visited on occasion and our relationship blossomed to some extent. We experienced some happier moments than in a long time. For over a year things went along fairly smooth. Then, Louis decided he didn't make enough money at the print shop and started working in a tattoo shop doing tattoos again. I wished he would use his excellent art talent some other way.

The element of people he associated with in the business brought him back to the drug scene, or else he went back himself and found association with them his desire. How do we know which happened first?

Shortly, he landed in prison again. From time to time he called and wanted money. Charles and I practiced tough love, something we grew familiar with concerning Louis. We found it necessary for our own peace of mind, lives, and survival. He hated it. He accused us of not loving him unconditionally.

"Yes, son, I love you unconditionally, but my blessings come with conditions. Like the Lord, He loves unconditionally, but his promises and blessings require stipulations." My response infuriated him. He never acknowledged or agreed with this thinking. Our relationship suffered and peaked from bad to worse over the years, depending on his frame of mind and drug and alcohol involvement. I loved my son, so the pain and heartaches grew intense. Things escalated and our relationship became broken.

Louis continued to live his life the way he wanted. He persisted in drinking and abusing drugs. The woman he chose to marry shared his lifestyle. They finally used up all their friends and relatives, and found themselves living on the streets. What a painful thing for me to even think about. Yet, I knew I could not help them until they were ready. I tried several times to get Louis, and once both of them, into programs such as Teen Challenge. Each time, he bolted. More than once, I had everything arranged only to have him run in another direction.

They ended up living on the streets of Austin, Texas, going from shelter to shelter. One night Louis's wife phoned. Louis landed in the hospital again. His admission nothing new, for the illnesses associated with his addictions brought him there often. He had developed diabetes, hepatitis C, cirrhosis of the liver and other health problems. I contemplated driving to Austin to visit him. Before I made up my mind or could do anything, I received another call from her.

"Louis is dead. While the doctors worked on his heart, it stopped." She reported in a matter of fact manner.

"No, no, tell me it's not true." I cried out in anguish.

"I don't know what you want me to tell you. Louis is dead." She repeated.

For the second time in my life, my heart flew into a million pieces. I thought it would never survive this blow. But God showed up as He always does with the promise that He won't give us more than we can bear. *No temptation has overtaken you but such as is common to man; and God is faithful, who will not allow you to be tempted beyond what you are able, but with the temptation will provide the way of escape also, so that you will be able to endure it.* 1 Corinthians 10:13 (KJV)

"Just have me cremated. It'll be cheaper on you that way" The words Louis repeated to me on occasion came to mind. We discussed this more than once.

"I can't do that, Louis." Time and time again I answered him.

"Then, just don't claim my body and let the state bury me." His usual comeback hurt to the bone. I knew someday I would most likely face this decision because of the life he led. Again, I could not. I determined to give him a proper burial.

Louis knew he wouldn't live long with the lifestyle he chose. I suspected I would bury him, instead of the other way around. Knowing this didn't make it any easier. Thirty-five was too young to die.

Charles and I had no insurance on him, mainly because we couldn't purchase any, due to his drug usage. We shipped his body back to Oklahoma to my hometown in order to bury him next to his brother. It seemed like Deja Vu. However, I told my friends and loved ones, "It doesn't get any easier the second time around."

His father refused to help with the funeral expenses, so Charles and I took the money out of our savings. Louis made choices I did not like or agree with, but I still loved him and would see he received a decent burial.

The pastor who conducted John's funeral did Louis's as well. He proved to be a great comfort to me. "Charlotte, even though Louis didn't live his life the way you would have liked, it wasn't your fault and it doesn't make you a bad parent. God's kids didn't listen to Him either and He is the best parent ever, and our example." His words meant so much. He will never know how they brought me peace.

In the days and months ahead, I grieved for my son – both my sons. I again went from denial to anger with Louis for living his life the way he did. At times, I blamed myself and wondered if I should have done things differently. Forgiveness for both Louis and myself came hard. However, I forgave both him and me.

I purchased a double headstone for my sons that read: "Brothers at rest". Those words brought comfort and continue to console me each time I visit their gravesite. My sons, finally at rest, no longer live a life of turmoil. God's presence never left me through the funeral and the days, months, and years ahead. He wrapped me in His arms of love whenever I needed Him. He continues to be there for me.

God helped my heart heal to the degree anyone's can when they've lost a child. He will do the same for others. When I think of Louis, I try to think of the good times we shared together. I remember those times when we enjoyed one another. I try not to dwell on the difficult times. When I feel sad, I turn to God and he comforts me. I think upon the hope I have of seeing Louis again. Then God will make all things right. We will have only good times together. There will be no mind-altering drugs or alcohol – only perfect peace.

After I emerged from the worst times of my grief, I wrote this poem for a parent who lost her son, and have shared it with others at this painful time in their lives. I share it again now.

A Mile In Your Shoes
By Charlotte Holt

I wish I could make your heart ache less.
I would like to help in your hour of distress.
I want to bring you comfort and rest.
I would like to send you my very best.

All I can say is, "I hurt for you."
I have walked a mile in your shoes.
I too lost my sons in their prime.
It still hurts after a long time.

Many try to help as best they can.
Most of them really don't understand.
The comfort they bring is still worthwhile.
Even though it is difficult to smile.

Trusting Him In Your Grief/Charlotte Holt

I come to you and reach out my hand.
If you should ever need a friend,
Just call on me and I will be there,
Anytime, day or night hour.

Somehow God has brought me through.
I know He'll do the same for you.
His grace is sufficient. It's true!
Even during the times when you feel blue.

When times come that you feel so sad.
Just think of all the wonderful times you had.
It's okay to keep a precious memory.
But don't hold on too tight, set him free.

There will be times it's hard to realize he's gone.
Sometimes you'll feel so empty and alone.
At other times you'll feel angry and so mad.
You'll think nothing could ever feel so bad.

Just remember, God knows your need.
He's been there in your same steed.
He lost His child like you and me.
But it all ended in victory!

Now our children are together with the 'Son of Man'.
Though it may be hard for us to understand.
God looks at death in a whole different way.
Someday we will too, I pray.

It's just the beginning and not the end.
For a whole new life will now begin.
It will last forever and a day.
I hope this thought will with you stay.

Charlotte Holt *retired from 30 years of teaching, author* *of* Praise The Lord for Roaches! And Anything Else That Bugs You. The Texas State Inspirational Writers Alive! elected her 'Writer of the Year' in 2002. *Her articles and poems appear online, in anthologies and magazines. She deposited two sons in Heaven but enjoys three stepchildren and three step grandchildren. Her greatest accomplishments entail knowing the Lord and being married for 32 years to Charles Holt, owner of North Houston Exterminators. They reside in Kingwood, Texas.*

Charlotte's Comments

Many people have told me this simple poem brought them comfort. I know God used it to help them through a rough time. That's why I feel compelled to bring you this book of encouragement from others and me in order to comfort and help heal your heart.

Prayer: *Lord, I pray the hearts of all those who read this book will be healed. May they find comfort in the pages and between them by those things only You and Your Spirit can say to them. I pray in Jesus Name. Amen.*

Chapter Twenty-Five
The Heartache of Losing a Child
By Evelyn Thompson

The heartache of losing a child is something a parent thinks they will never get over. But the Lord gives peace that passes understanding.

This is how it was when we lost our daughter, Shelley. God showed us we were blessed to have her for forty years. What a joy she was during that time. Always smiling, very active in everything. I talked to her everyday. My husband and I still laugh at times and say, "Isn't that just like Shelley."

Shelley was diagnosed with diabetes at the age of nine. It came as a shock to us because she looked happy and healthy. We began giving her shots and kept her on a special diet. It hurt me to stick her, but that was her life. She knew how it hurt me. She took it all in stride. She was a beautiful little girl.

Years passed and Shelley grew active in her church. She loved life. She graduated from high school with good grades. She wanted to get a job so we bought her a car, in order for her to find one. We were so proud of her. She was a special young lady.

Time marched on and Shelley and her high school sweetheart told us they wanted to get married. Happiness radiated from them at the wedding we gave them. After three years of marriage they wanted a child. Shelley had to watch her insulin, but they were blessed by the arrival of their son, William. The doctor advised her not to have another child. Shelley accepted this, as always, in stride. She took one of her bedrooms and filled it with computers and everything she needed, so she could work at home and be with her son.

When William graduated from high school, we were so proud of him, especially Shelley. He turned out to be a fine and handsome fellow.

Shelley called me one night and talked for two hours.

"How can you find so much to say?" my husband, Charley, said. This being a Saturday we got off the phone to get ready for church on Sunday.

After church we went to the cafeteria to eat. We stood waiting in line at Luby's when Shelley's brother-in-law walked in and told us something was wrong. Shelley was in the hospital unable to breath on her own. We were stunned.

She attended a different church from ours. An

evangelist spoke that day and prayed for people at the end of the service. Shelley helped take the elderly people down to the altar. When he finished praying for everyone, he addressed Shelley. "Would you like for me to pray for you?"

"I am so tired of taking shots and I want the Lord to heal me." Following her statement she fell. She lay there a long time, and someone finally lifted up her head. Her breathing had stopped. When we arrived at the hospital, we found out she experienced a massive heart attack.

Our hearts broke to hear this news. We went into shock, but the Lord saw us through the difficult days ahead. We knew she was with Him. We were thankful she lived long enough to see her son graduate from high school. We are grateful for so many things, and the times we spent together with her.

One Monday, September 25, 1995, a few hours after my husband and I went to bed, I had a dream, or vision. The Lord must have wanted to comfort me. I stood inside a building with sliding windows. I saw my beloved daughter walking toward me across the way. She held her car keys in her hand along with some papers and books. A picture I saw hundreds of times during her life with us. I called out to her. "Shelley, Shelley."

She went inside the building. I tried to open the sliding window while yelling her name. The back of her head revealed the most beautiful long wavy auburn hair, like that of an angel. Finally, I got her attention and she came into the building with us. We laughed and talked about things we had shared together. Then we walked into this big closet. Toy dolls and all sorts of things I made for her filled it to the ceiling. We laughed again. Then I asked if I could hold her.

"I think that would be all right with me," she said.

Apparently, I saw these things in the spiritual realm, for Shelley went to be with the Lord August 10, 1994. You can imagine how upset my husband was when I woke him crying and sobbing. I scared him because I couldn't tell him why I cried – until I got control of myself.

When I did, Charley held me and wiped away my tears. The Lord had comforted me by allowing me one last good time with Shelley. He gave me Charley to help me in my grief. One way or another He sees us through our difficult times and brings us peace, for He is the God of all comfort.

Even though we know our grieving will never completely end here on earth, we know He is there in the midst of it and He will hold our hand. We have a hope that we will see her again and then we can laugh and talk forever.

Evelyn Thompson was born in Indianapolis, Indiana. She lived in Porter, Texas with her husband of 40 years. She and her husband, Charlie, started as friends and remained friends. You saw them everywhere together. They loved their church and ministered in various capacities – greeters, ushers, servers, photographer and whatever they could do to help anyone. They were a blessing to all who knew them. Besides Shelley, Evelyn had one other child, Steven. Evelyn has gone home to be with her Savior and Shelley. They have begun their forever of laughing and talking. Her husband Charlie still serves his church.

Charlotte's Comments

If we will look to the good times with our child, as this mother has done, we will find peace. We will find joy again. If we will open our hearts to those around us, who need us and want us in their lives, we can have a full life.

We must not hang onto our past too tightly if we wish to live in the present and look to the future. The present is actually the only time we have. The past is over and the future has not yet come. Don't miss out on living. Live in the present.

"God how can I ever let go of my loved one? He was my life." I've heard others remark.

"Dear ones, our life has changed, it will never be the same again. They are gone. There is nothing we can do to change it, but we can live our lives today. Determine to move on. God will open new opportunities. He will give more than we ever dared hope, think, or dream." I assure them of a new life in Him.

We never stop missing our loved ones, but we must live our lives until we join them and Him. We must trust Him in our grief.

Prayer: *Lord, help us to live the full life You have for us. Help us to live in the present. We thank You that someday we will see our child, or children, again. Thank You for the opportunities You give us each day. In Jesus Name. Amen.*

Chapter Twenty-Six
Prayers
By Charlotte Maxwell

From the first time I became a mom to the last time, my prayer before going to sleep was "God watch over my children and keep them safe." I birthed a daughter and then three sons. My youngest, Kevin, came almost five years after his middle brother. I believe he felt left out of the closeness of the older three.

In fourth grade Kevin had problems in public school, so I placed them both in a church school. Kevin lived in the shadow of his popular brother who did everything right. The school rules were ridged and Kevin stayed in trouble most of the time. He developed feelings of inferiority and started drugging and drinking in his teens. Raised in church, he wanted to please. He maintained somewhat of a relationship with God. By the grace of God, he did eventually overcome his addictions and became again the son I knew as a child.

When Kevin drank, we had a shaky relationship and I didn't always treat him with kindness. My disgust outweighed my compassion. I thought he just needed to straighten up and fly right. I later learned addiction can often be stronger than the person and only God can set him free. In the end God did restore the years the locusts had eaten and He gave us a good relationship. Only God can do this.

After my children grew into adults and moved out on their own, I didn't pray that prayer of protection as often. Kevin lived in a complex of four freestanding apartments in a quad.

On a fatal Sunday night, I received the call that constitutes every mother's worst nightmare. Kevin and his nephew heard a commotion outside Kevin's apartment. They walked outside to check out the noise. A young man brutally abused his wife. My son confronted him and tried to stop him. The man turned on Kevin and stabbed him with a kitchen knife.

My grandson made the call. "Grandma, they've taken Kevin to the hospital." He filled in some of the details.

We rushed down there but they wouldn't let us see him. After what seemed like an eternity, about two hours, they took us into a room and a team of doctors told us Kevin had lost too much blood and would not survive.

When we finally saw him, he was on life support and stayed on it for about sixteen hours. I prayed God would let him live, but He had other plans.

My great sense of disappointment in God overwhelmed me. I screamed at Him, "Where were You and how could You have let this happen?"

For some time after Kevin died I couldn't talk to God. I could only kneel at the chair where I usually prayed and say, "God I can't think of anything to say to You."

God would fill the whole room with his love and I felt as though he had His arms around me, a sensation so strong I could almost reach out and touch Him.

I realized God had been right there when my son died. God hadn't moved away from any of us. I read a dozen or more books on grief. I tried to make sense of it all. Kevin's death at the young age of 35 didn't make sense to me no matter how hard I tried. Then someone shared a Scripture from Isaiah 57:1,2 —*The righteous perish, and no one ponders it in his heart; devout men are taken away, and no one understands that the righteous are taken away to be spared from evil. Those who walk uprightly enter into peace; they find rest as they lie in death.* Okay, I could accept that. The words comforted me.

Ten months after Kevin's death, his father died. In my mind, I imagined Kevin meeting his dad and saying, "Come on in, Dad, let me show you around. Let's go see Jesus."

I have never experienced, or ever will experience, anything as painful as Kevin's death. Yet, I had, also, never known the love of God so strong and so close. God has blessed me with many more family members and enough love to help me not to succumb to hopelessness. God is good and He remains my rock and my salvation.

When I faced the subject of forgiveness, I said, "WHAT!" Surely God didn't expect me to forgive the man who murdered my son. But He did. The Bible teaches if we are to be forgiven, we must forgive. I knew it was not humanly possible for me to forgive in and of myself, and I had to depend on God's forgiveness to work through me. Forgiveness sets us free. So as an act of my will, whether I wanted to or not, I did forgive. The young man received twenty-five years for murdering my son. Is that enough to pay for a son's life? No, I don't think so. Even though I have forgiven I still want justice. But that too is up to God. I do pray he will find peace with God, give his heart to Him, and be the man God created him to be.

Charlotte Maxwell *was born in Houston, Texas in 1938 and moved to the Humble area at an early age. She completed the eleventh grade at Aldine. She married the love of her life, Robert, and had four beautiful children. Attending church all her life, she chose to raise her* *children in the same manner. She attends Humble First Assembly.*

Charlotte's Comments

Losing a child is always difficult but to lose one at the hands of someone else must be even harder. Only God can help someone forgive that person. Charlotte knew she must forgive in order to find peace. Yes, we are forgiven in the same measure we forgive. Even the Lord's Prayer acknowledges this principal when we say, "Forgive us our trespasses as we forgive those who trespass against us." Many Scriptures throughout the Bible let's us know how important forgiveness is. When we harbor unforgiveness for anyone—ourselves, God, or others, we hurt ourselves. Through the process of forgivenes, we become better instead of bitter.

Prayer: *Father, we thank You for helping us forgive, even when we find it difficult. You know the healing it brings. Thank You for forgiving us of our sins. Thank You for dying on the cross so we might experience the peace and joy the process brings into our lives. We know You paid a terrible price to bring us to the place where we can be forgiven and so we can forgive. Help us to continue walking in forgiveness in our daily lives one* step at a time. Help us to always forgive in the same way we are forgiven. In Jesus Name. Amen.

Chapter Twenty-Seven
The Grief Experience of a Father
By Charles Girling
With Pat Girling and Suzanne Merrifield

My beautifully "normal" days were forever changed when my first-born daughter, Claire, was killed in a car wreck at age 39. A dump truck's brakes failed at a red light and she was gone in a moment, which altered all the days ahead. She left three children ages 6, 9 and 16 at the time of her death. My own grief was difficult enough, but it was multiplied and intensified by knowing the pain and loss felt by her husband and children.

Both then and now her death was difficult to accept. I remember upon first hearing the news I asked her husband three times in disbelief, "Are you sure ..." "Are you sure it was Claire?"

My family and I have since talked at length about why it is so difficult to comprehend that she isn't going to walk through our door again someday. My younger daughter, Suzanne suggested that perhaps it is difficult to grasp an end to life since our soul is eternal and was not created by God with the intention of an end.

The separation of death came as a result of sin, but originally we were meant to live eternally with God.

Even in our fallen existence, our souls will live on …
eternally. And so, maybe this "eternal" hard wiring into
our human bodies makes death a strange concept to
grasp. I think this insight may, at least partially explain,
why I occasionally still want to pick up the phone and
call Claire, even though she's been gone almost eight
years now.

Scripture says God chose death for this life over
an eternal separation. Seeing death as protection from
something worse brings purpose and understanding for
awful earthly grief.

Knowing that I will be with Claire eternally
brings anticipation of the day when I will get to be with
her again. Theology, thoughts, Scriptures and prayer
helps us deal with our grief, not deny it. I think it's the
"hope." Thinking about, imagining being with her again
is exciting.

My youngest daughter, Jacquelyn, only four
years old at the time, drew a picture of Claire and a
flower. The flower was about 100 times bigger than the
simple stick figure – Claire. If a child can imagine this, it
shows we cannot conceive what is coming. This thought
inspired the "idea" of Claire sleeping in the middle of a
HUGE flower … the flower center … a round cushy

"king size" mattress and Claire enjoying a beautiful peaceful rest inside this fabulous room-sized flower.

This image of a heavenly garden beyond my wildest imaginations ministered such joy since I am myself a gardener. The love that I have for Claire merged with my love of flowers and beauty brought peace to an even greater level. I think that healing came from the Lord in a form that I could fully appreciate - a rose garden. Wow, I never even imagined a flower that big!

I have heard stories of fathers who have a hard time saying, "I love you" to their children and after a child's death wondering *did she know how much I loved her?* I must say that I am so glad I do not have to feel that sadness and regret. The first month after her death, it seemed life stood totally still. We did not run from that time but tried to embrace it. I remember how good it felt, in those otherwise terrible moments knowing Claire and I had such a good relationship. I will always miss her. I still miss her. I am glad beyond words that I told her often "I love you" and I know that she knew how much I loved her.

I am not implying in anyway that she and I had a Norman Rockwell life. She was not a perfect daughter, I was not a perfect father but our love for one another was never a question. Love covers many faults. In our family we tried to deal with the reality of our sins and weaknesses so that we could bring these areas out into the open, allowing healing and restoration. A relationship is not about proving yourself right or wrong, or being perfect but about asking for and giving, truth, mercy and grace to deal with our weaknesses and turn them into strengths.

Many people believe in "unconditional" love, but I believe that sincere love has boundaries. Claire was such a great example of someone who pursued the purity of love and truth. If she thought conflict could bring about positive change for something she believed was right or important, she would go there. She did not like to have conflict, but she was willing if necessary. She had strong convictions and you could count on Claire to stand up for what she believed was right. To her "love" was right.

She was an incredible teacher. As a matter of fact, on the day she was killed, she was on her way home from graduate class, where she was pursuing a career as a college level instructor. She wanted to make a difference, especially in young people's lives, and was diligent in her God-given mission. She was highly honored by her college for her outstanding contribution, even though she was only in the early stages of teaching at that level. She thought she had not even begun.

It was amazing how much the Lord honored her life and how many people were blessed just talking about her during our time of heaviest grief. Conversations about her, even to strangers, brought all of us comfort and peace. We learned that the way you live is the way you truly are remembered. I love thinking about her when she was alive. I remember many wonderful memories. The pain of her loss has never gone away and never will. But the joy of knowing her never has and never will either.

Learning to do things in her memory has helped us get through. Our first Christmas without her happened only two months after her death and we tried to think of what Claire would want us to do. Our feelings tempted us to give up joy and celebration but we chose instead to honor her by giving the gift of joy and celebration to hers and all of the children in the family and ultimately to ourselves.

Choosing to honor the memory of Claire gave us the power to continue to make the holiday a happy time.

Because children don't grieve the way adults do they cannot understand the depth of the loss. A child lives in the present so their "let's play no mater what" ministers to your spirit to keep living. That does not mean you should deny the grief, but let the grief intensify what matters – how important loving each other is … saying, "I love you" and enjoying the small moments.

One comment Clair's mother-in-law made when we gathered together for the funeral was, "It will never be the same." Time has proven her right. During grief, good and bad feelings seem more intense. Sounds seem louder; lights seem brighter, feeling deeper. What really matters is looked at more closely, when you suddenly become aware we were together - just a "normal family gathering."

Though we knew Claire's life was clearly a Christ-centered life and she was with Him eternally, it was still a great loss to us. We have grieved deeply and embraced the healing that has come, although there are scars and life will never be the same.

Even after all this time the loss is still deep and laced with strong emotion. The loss never goes away in this life, and maybe we understand things better because of our pain. If even Christ suffered, maybe the purpose of pain has eternal value. We are told in Scripture that we understand in part. We do not know all the answers now. I am glad that means there is more to anticipate than we can even imagine.

My hope for eternity does not lessen or minimize the reality and joys of this life, but makes me know great things are yet to come. If you can't enjoy the journey why make the trip?

Can grief be enjoyed? Probably not – embraced? Maybe. Loving Claire was knowing Claire. Losing Claire is still loving Claire. That is living at its best.

We are not human beings having a spiritual experience. We are spiritual beings having a human experience ~ Teilhard de Chardin.

Charles M. and Pat Girling reside in Kingwood, TX. Thirty-three years of marriage, they have worked together professionally as well as in ministry to friends, family and church. Charles was born in Holmesville, MS and holds a Master's Degree in Horticulture. He was Regional Manager for Girling Health Care for twenty-four years.

Pat Wright Girling was born in Houston, TX to mission's ministry singing family. She has worked as a designer, jobs director, hairdresser, Special Project and Event Coordinator for Girling Health Care, Art/Production Director of magazine and creator of elaborate Christening gowns. Combined they have six children, eleven grandchildren and three great-grand daughters. They have had a child at home spanning 54 years for Charles and 41 years for Pat.

SuZanne Merrifield, *daughter, graduated from Dallas Baptist University with a B.S. in Education, GPA of 4.0. She married on New Year's Day in 1994. She is proud to call herself a Farmer's Wife and lives on the family farm in Dallas, TX with her husband and their two sons. She has an established career working in the health care industry. She enjoys and excels in painting, writing, creating her blog, reading, and cooking. SuZanne was six when Pat married Charles.*

Charlotte's Comments

Yes, we grieve and we can't believe our child is gone. I think disbelief is the first reaction and stage a parent, who has lost a child, experiences. There are still times, years later, when we expect them to walk through the door. We often think we see them on the street - if not them, someone who favors them.

When I notice someone who looks like one of my children, I tell myself he is not my son. Yet, it brings back a flood of memories. Sometimes it makes me sad, but most often I think of the good times. I experience sadness when I initially realize it is not my child and he is gone from me until I reach eternity. But, then, when I think of seeing him again in eternity, I know it will be forever. I will be with both my sons always and we will never be separated again. This brings comfort and joy. I know many of you must experience these same feelings. I hope comfort and joy comes to you as well.

Charles said it well. Knowing them – we love them. Losing them – we still love them. The love a parent feels for a child never ceases. Our heavenly Father, God, shows us this by His example. He loves us no matter. I believe that is true unconditional love. No matter how good or bad they are, no matter how much they hurt or disappoint us, no matter how far away they travel, no matter – we still love them because they are a part of us. They are our children!

Prayer: *Thank You for giving us our children. Thank You for Your unconditional love toward us. Thank You for the pain. Thank You for being there with us through the pain. Thank You for the beautiful lives you entrusted to us for a time. We thank You that we will see our children again and next time it will be forever. Lord, I ask You to bring comfort to every parent's heart as they remember their child. I ask that Your love over ride all the pain. In Jesus Name. Amen.*

Chapter Twenty-Eight
The Light of Sorrow
By Mary-Alice Wightman

Christmas excitement filled the air in our home. It blended with the fragrance of holiday foods, warm and inviting.

Our anticipation for this special Christmas was high with surprises we had made for our family. Bill had fashioned wooden trays in his workshop, and I made colorful booklets of flowers and poetry for keepsakes. Among the many decorations from our years together, a small new tree, bright with miniature snowmen, awaited our two great-grandsons.

The ringing of the phone cut into the laughing and chattering as all sixteen of us, representing four generations, assembled at the two tables extended as one. The call was for our granddaughter-in-law with the tragic message that her grown brother, Jeff, named the same as our third and youngest child, had died suddenly.

The startling message subdued all of us. I admired Susan's brave composure. Though obviously upset, she insisted on staying through dinner and the gift time for the sake of her three-year old son. I felt as if a pall had come over us, yet with genuine sympathy everyone tried to keep the evening festive. Only later would I think of this as a somber omen.

My New Year's resolution was to finally do our Jeff's scrapbook, having already completed those for our older children. January was pleasantly filled with gathering and sorting all the keepsakes and pictures to tell his story. An overflowing box of mementoes waited when February arrived. Suddenly I felt as if a dark cloud loomed over me. It weighed heavy with unfounded depression.

I was still feeling sad and uneasy the morning of February 16, as we drove to the doctor's office for my husband's checkup. Since his kidney surgery almost three years before, there had been many checkups. Several times tumors had to be removed from the bladder. What a great relief – no tumors this time. The cloud was lifted and I reasoned that my worry about Bill's health had brought on my depression those recent weeks.

Soon after lunch the phone at home rang.

"Jeff's plane has crashed in Pueblo, Colorado…no survivors." The voice on the other end stated.

Our Jeff, 42, was co-pilot of the flight with six passengers that left Richmond for California that morning. The stark tragedy hit us like a nightmare.

We screamed and cried in disbelief, clinging to each other and sobbing, "No! No!"

We loved him so much. Jeff was extremely happy in his flying and in his marriage of less than two years. His wife, Jean, would be coming in the door soon, and we felt we had to hold up for her sake. We also had to begin notifying the family and help make arrangements.

Our minister was most compassionate and helpful in carrying out Jeff's Memorial Service, as Jean felt appropriate. A huge crowd overflowed the sanctuary on the Sunday afternoon following the evening of visitation at the funeral home. People of all ages waited in line to pay their respects

For days visitors filled our home with their love and sympathy and an abundance of food and flowers. I could feel the strength of their prayers, which kept me strong to greet and comfort others who felt as sad and shocked as we did. Knowing how much all of this meant to my family, I gladly attended the service for the pilot with whom Jeff was flying. It served as a reminder that I was not the only one suffering from this tragedy. This was difficult but God gave me the strength to be with another family in the sorrow I knew.

Jeff always had a wonderful warm smile. Now more friends, than seemed possible for him to have known, came. All of them expressed their love and admiration for him. We felt proud of our son who had matured into a fine young man. He brought love and laughter into our lives every day. It did not seem right for me to complain about losing him so young.

His contagious smile shown in the picture beside the "airplane flower arrangement" at his service kept me smiling. Jean and our daughter chose beautiful hymns appropriate for the Memorial. I chose "Love Lifted Me", which has always lifted my spirits in troubled times. In love and gratitude now, I truly felt that no matter how great our loss, our blessings from having shared Jeff's life were greater.

With others wondering how I could accept this accident, I realized God had given me those dark weeks I had not understood in early February, perhaps for a reason. Could it possibly have served as a pre-grieving time so that I could absorb the shock of the loss when it came, enabling me to remain strong for others during that time? Whatever the explanation, I am thankful and my trust in God continues to grow with deeper appreciation.

That trust helped us through two of the toughest times of our sorrowful ordeal. The first hurdle was the long week waiting for Jeff to "come home."

Bill chose to welcome him in his heart at our house. At the funeral parlor that night my daughter and I went in first. We respected Jean's wish to say her good-bye in private after we left. We did not stay long. There was nothing gentle in the stark reality of the bare cardboard box. Horrendous! Janet and I hugged it and cried, longing to see Jeff's gentle face, remembering his dear features at their best. Jean had her time, leaving a yellow tulip in remembrance.

The next hurdle was the "fly over" to spread the ashes at the river as we felt Jeff would want. A group of fifty friends and family gathered on the shore at noon on the Saturday planned. However, the sky was too overcast for the low flying plane to be safe. Covered dishes were brought so this became a time of fellowship with Jeff's buddies cooking on the grill, as he loved to do. Time together to talk was healing for all of us.

Later the next week when the weather

Trusting Him In Your Grief/Charlotte Holt

cooperated, a smaller group of fifteen stood on the beach as the plane flew over, circling back around, releasing the ashes. They appeared in the blue sky like a thin light red material, gracefully forming into shapes as if lingering in a loving good-bye. Suddenly the vision seemed to evaporate, vanishing in mid-air. In the silence of death, my heart's pain was bittersweet, feeling our loss while feeling assured Jeff was safe with God.

I walked to the edge of the river and placed the red rose, I had been holding, on the water to float out with the tide. Somehow this symbolized for me the lifelong love of a mother/child bond. That bonding begins before birth and continues beyond death. I have loved Jeff all of his life, and I will continue to love him all of my life.

Whenever our hearts seem heavier than we can bear we realize, as parents, that we have known a fuller measure of our child's love than many other parents ever received. We thank God for that precious gift – a love great enough to compensate for the pain of our loss. Of course, we cannot deny the great void Jeff left but talking about him often and laughing at special memories brings us comfort.

We try to keep busy, avoiding an excess of tears.

Yet, we are not moving like robots without feelings. God gives us the armor to shield us from dwelling on our sorrow. That protection comes through the love and goodness of people He puts in our lives.

So many wonderful happenings amaze us: a visit from the minister who christened Jeff at two months old, notes and calls from long-time friends from out of town, visits from the president of the airlines, pilot's wives setting up a fund for them to be matched by the airline, condolences on the internet from neighbors from Jeff's childhood as well as new friends who had just met Jeff a few months earlier, a special card from an aunt of one of the crash victims from Utah.

One that really touched me was a gift for Mothers' Day. The lovely azalea filled with pink blooms came with a card.

"We remember, too, from a friend of Jeff's because I know he would have wanted to send his Mother a gift."

Jean has been a beautiful blessing to us through the months and we have tried to be there for her without intruding. She continues to be like a daughter, another gift to us from God – and from Jeff!

The past has also blessed us with a gift in the example of our parents. Watching them remain strong through illness and loss has ingrained within us their sustaining strength. Even though, we miss Jeff every day, there is the "light of sorrow", a beam of hope that brightens the way for love and joy within our hearts. No matter how dim it may begin, this light is for everyone. Unlike our bodies, which grow weaker through the years, our spirits grow stronger with love throughout our lives. Thanks be to God for the strength that faith in Him provides.

Mary-Alice Wightman, 78, is a homemaker. She enjoys traveling, reading and writing. She has published two books of poetry and co-authored the book, Come Live With Me. Mary has published poems in Tennessee Voices, Ideals Magazine, Grandmother Earth, and Poetry Society of Virginia Anthology of Poems. She has two children, three grandchildren, and two great grandsons. Mary-Alice and her husband, Bill, live in Mechanicsville, Virginia, where they are active in their church.

Charlotte's Comments

Mary-Alice mentioned that talking about Jeff helped them. I believe this is something too often overlooked by sympathetic loved ones. They don't know how to handle our talking about our deceased child. It makes them sad, and they don't know what to say. Little do they realize our lost loved one was a big part of our life and their memories remain sweet to us.

Of course, it is not good if a parent talks excessively about their lost child either. Our lives must go on to the present and the future. We cannot live in the past with our child. However, it is healthy to remember the things they did, what they liked to eat, special times with them in the same way we do with our living children. They occupied a large part of our lives and naturally we should remember and talk about them.

I pray those of you who are listeners will remember that the next time a parent brings up something their lost child did, who they were, or even what they liked. Parents shouldn't expect everyone to carry on a lengthy conversation about their lost child, but acknowledging they lived and breathed by listening helps a great deal.

On the other hand, parents, it is best to share our memories of our child with those who feel comfortable doing so. My husband and I share things about my sons on occasion and both enjoy the remembrances. However, we do not share them with total strangers or people who feel ill at ease with it. We need to choose our listeners when sharing about our child. Like anything else, we don't share everything with everyone.

The things Mary-Alice saw as God's special gifts warmed my heart, and I hope it did others. God resides in the midst of our storms to comfort, console, and bless us, if we will just look for Him and His gifts and miracles.

It has only been a short time since Mary-Alice lost Jeff. I believe she is doing remarkably well – the reason being – she has trusted Him in her grief! If we will continue to do so, He will see us through in victory.

Prayer: *Lord, I pray You will continue to console, comfort and bless those who have suffered this intense sorrow of losing a child. Let us all look for the gifts and miracles You provide and accept them as from You. Help us be sensitive to our audience when discussing our child or children and please show them how to listen to our heart's cries. May we all be in tune with You and Your will for each of our lives. Once we trust our lives to You we will never be the same again, and once we lose a child the same holds true. Help us to trust You in our grief. In Jesus Name. Amen.*

Chapter Twenty-Nine
Louisa Ann Krunchenberg
By Louis E. McVey

Our child, whom we loved very much, was born January 2, 1950. We were thankful God lent her to us until February 15, 1996. We got to keep her with us for 46 years. She was not a young child when she died, but children are supposed to bury their parents, not the other way around.

In 1970, the Mayo Clinic in Minnesota discovered Louisa had a cancerous tumor in her stomach area. They operated and told us they had removed it all. However, in 1990, they found a tumor on her brain. She went through many surgeries until 1996 when she passed away.

Louisa Ann was a loving child. She loved children though she was never able to have any of her own. One of the memories that will always stick with me happened one day in her home. She was baking sugar cookies for her nieces and nephews. After baking a few cookies she would place them on the table to cool. When she turned her back the children would take three or four and eat them until they were gone. Then she would bake

275

more. The same thing happened over and over. We try to keep these good memories alive in our hearts.

God takes the memories and sifts them through His great love. We don't dwell on the times of pain and suffering she endured. We try to keep the good memories ever before us. The word of God tells us to think on the good things. *Finally, brethren, whatever is true, whatever is honorable, whatever is right, whatever is pure, whatever is lovely, whatever is of good repute, if there is any excellence and if anything worthy of praise, dwell on these things.* Philippians 4:8 (NASB)

When she passed away she was working at a place taking care of mentally ill children. We were proud of her and all she accomplished. She attended two years of Bible school before she dropped out due to her illness. No matter her pain, discomfort, disappointments, she always kept a smile on her face. There came a time when the cancer left her unable to talk. I would get up to her ear and tell her how much I loved her and she would smile. I knew she could still hear me, and it pleased me to be able to let her know of our great love for her.

During the time of her illness and death, we always kept the faith. We knew she would want us to depend on the Lord. She had, through each suffering moment. Up to the end she thought of others. She never wanted to be a bother to anyone.

We knew God was there and we continued to pray. Still today, the grief comes, even after all these years, so we pray, think on the good things and times and remember we have the blessed hope. Having that hope, we know we will see her again and next time it will be more than 46 years – It will be forever!

For if we believe that Jesus died and rose again, even so God will bring with Him those who have fallen asleep in Jesus. For this we say to you by the word of the Lord, that we who are alive and remain until the coming of the Lord, will not precede those who have fallen asleep. For the Lord Himself will descend from heaven with a shout, with the voice of {the} archangel and with the trumpet of God, and the dead in Christ will rise first. Then we who are alive and remain will be caught up together with them in the clouds to meet the Lord in the air, and so we shall always be with the Lord. Therefore comfort one another with these words. 1 Thessalonians 4:14-18 (NASB)

Louis McVey and his wife, Merriam, were born in Illinois but resided in Kingwood, Texas. They were the proud parents of two other children, Bradley McVey and Dianna Johnson. They were blessed with six grandchildren and a great grand child. They loved the Lord and belonged to the First Assembly of God Church in Humble, Texas, where Louis was an usher. He has gone on home to be with his Savior and Louisa.

Charlotte's Comments

No matter the age of a child, it is difficult to lose them. They are supposed to bury us, as Louis said, not us them. These parents loved their child with all their heart. I watched tears form in their eyes when they spoke of her, but the stories they shared brought back fond memories. They had only good things to say in regard to her. They missed her very much. However, they went on with their lives to help others in need in whatever way they could.

Prayer: *Father, I pray for Your comfort for each parent as they continue to miss their child or children. Help us all to always remember the stories that keep us close to our child. Help us to use what we have gone through in the loss of a child to help and minister to others in need. Give us a soft heart of empathy towards our fellow sufferers instead of a hard and bitter heart. I pray in Jesus Name. Amen.*

Chapter Thirty
Thanks for the Memory
As told to Denise H. McEwen
By Phyllis Huff

Wednesday morning, August 20, 2003 began as an ordinary day. I talked with my son, Richard on the telephone as I did most mornings. We had one of the best conversations I could remember in a long time.

"You must show people what to do, otherwise things won't get done," he enthusiastically stated as he spoke about motivating people when working on projects. He took charge and led a team of people he worked with to a successful finish.

He also spoke of his sisters and related how fortunate he felt to have them. I hung up the telephone and continued my morning routine. With nothing on my calendar that day, I took my time getting dressed.

BAM, BAM, BAM! A constant banging came. I bolted to the front door. By the time I opened it I saw Richard's wife, Kim, running back to her car.

"Kim!" I called to her. She stopped, turned in a panic towards me and yelled, "Richard's had a heart attack…I can't drive."

Trusting Him In Your Grief/Charlotte Holt

I finished dressing but took no time for makeup. I drove Kim to pick up Austin, their oldest son, at his sixth grade campus. Silence enveloped the car. Blank stares, questions flooded my mind, dotted with spaces of numbness. I couldn't imagine the things going through Kim's mind.

She called the local Christian radio station asking for prayers. Then a call came from my husband, Lynn. He waited at the hospital and grappled with the bad news alone. He wanted to make sure we didn't rush to the hospital. He cautioned us to drive safely.

"We should slow down," Kim said quietly staring straight ahead. Our eyes locked and in that moment I knew my son no longer lived on this earth. We remained silent, not wanting Austin to know just yet.

I went from wondering to complete shock. I knew I would never see my son again so full of life and joy as when we talked earlier that morning.

When we arrived at the hospital, I stayed with Richard until the medical examiner came five hours later, completely unaware of what went on outside or around me. Grief enfolded me and I began a deep journey into my soul. I wondered if I would ever recover from my own wounded heart.

"You have your memories," someone told me. The words rang out like a rusty gong. *Good intentions misplaced at such a critical time.*

"He's better off," others said.

Dumbfounded, I remembered the times I said such things to help others in their grief. I wondered if I meant well or tried to satisfy my discomfort. In any case, I asked forgiveness.

Phyllis, what DO you want to hear instead? Came the make-believe interrogation from the pure hearts, which unknowingly caused more pain.

Nothing! I said to myself in silent frustration. I wanted to hear nothing at that moment. No one can speak the perfect words to sum up the life of your child. Only God holds the power to do so.

Time stretched from seconds to minutes and then into days, slowly becoming a year. Life struts along at its own pace oblivious to the world's pain, unable to correct any tragedy, which took place within its walls.

Eighteen months later I sat in my weekly lady's Bible class. Pam, Kim's sister spoke. Her oldest son, Nolan, a dedicated athlete on his way to college the next year wanted to relate a story of one of his experiences.

My mind wandered back almost thirty years.

Richard, a fine athlete himself, was born with a heart condition called mitral valve prolapse. The doctors, always reluctant and cautious to release him to play organized sports, allowed and encouraged him to take part in regular physical education. He wanted desperately to play football. So, off we went to his current cardiologist. We made the five hour drive full of anticipation and hope.

"You will never be able to participate in sports," the doctor said. "You will have to make a living with your brain."

With those words Richard's athletic fate became sealed. My heart sank as I watched Richard's face drop. We made the five-hour drive back. Richard sat silently looking out the window the whole time. I could do nothing.

Back in lady's class, Pam began her story.

"At his latest baseball game I became upset because Nolan didn't get to play enough. I noticed his positive attitude. After the game he walked our way. He looked spry and as if he felt great. 'How did you feel when the coach didn't put you in when he could have?' I asked."

"Mom," Nolan said with a smile, "I thought of

Uncle Richard and what he would do. I knew he'd feel good and I realized I could do the same. It's all good."

It's all good. Richard's catch phrase the last few months before he died came rushing back to me. He would smile as big as Texas and say, "It's all good," whenever something challenging happened.

Thoughts still flood my mind today. I find that what seemed impossible to understand eighteen months ago brings comfort to me now.

"You've got your memories." Several people said these words to me when my heart felt ripped wide open and I stood exposed and vulnerable. Yet, somehow the words had a different affect this time. A truth I could not swallow then, today, I embrace completely. They can't replace Richard but they do have value.

Nolan's story kept revolving in my mind. Here is a young man who is influenced in so many ways by my son. He is especially influenced in the area of organized sports, something Richard only dreamed of doing.

My ultimate comfort comes from knowing my son is with God now. God gave me a gift because Richard still lives on in the memories of others and continues to influence their decisions even now.

Phyllis Huff *lives in Magnolia, Texas with her husband,*

Lynn. They have been married for 56 years. They have three children, Denise H. McEwen, Richard Huff, at home with the Lord, and Andreia Dippon. Phyllis and Lynn were missionaries in São Paulo, Brazil for 13 years building and directing a youth camp called Camp Mount of Olives. She and Lynn serve the church of Christ on Buckshot Lane in Magnolia, TX where Lynn is the pulpit minister and Phyllis teaches women's classes.

Denise H. *McEwen has written for church bulletins, contributed to a quarterly women's newsletter and she now serves where she is needed in her home congregation. She and her husband, John, have been married 18 years. Denise grew up on the mission field in Brazil. She has written devotionals and Bible studies for women and children's classes. She was a member of Words for the Journey Writer's Guild in The Woodlands, Texas until she moved to the San Antonio area.*

Charlotte's Comments

Yes, Phyllis, we have our memories. They remain precious to us. I find as time goes on and God heals my heart, the memories become sweeter and I chose to remember the good times. Instead of remembering the hurt and pain of our children's death, we should try to remember the great times we had together: the times we played a game together, the Christmases we spent opening gifts and taking down Santa socks, the meals we shared together, the fishing trips, the baseball games, our children's favorite movies or food. The list could continue on. These are the priceless things our television tells us about in commercials.

One of the funniest memories I have of my son, John, entails the way he loved a large Christmas stocking. One year I bought him the biggest sock I could find in the store. Measuring about his height, he held it up with a huge smile on his face. He really expected Santa to fill it to the brim – and he did. I can still see the gigantic sock and the look on John's face when he saw it on Christmas morning.

Another memory that stands out consists of the day John and his stepsister, Valerie, prepared dinner for my husband and me. Afterwards they put on a puppet show for us. I think it surely provided us with the best entertainment ever.

I still remember the time Louis brought me roses home from the store where he worked. Even though he only made a sacker's wage, he spent some of his hard earned money on roses for me. It still touches my heart and brings tears of joy to my eyes.

Memories flood my mind of each of my boys as I think on these things. I'm sure all of us, who have lost children, can remember those precious times. We can even remember the hard times and know God has worked them for our good. We can know He is God of the valleys and God of the mountaintops. He occupied all the places we have walked. He walked beside us and held our hands. He continues to be there in our times of grief and He has set us free from mourning. He has helped us take off the sackcloth and ashes.

He can and will do the same for any who will turn to and depend upon Him. Our memories can be precious and our mourning can turn to dancing. Turn lose of the pain and allow the memories to take you to a new height with God.

Prayer: *Lord, help us to give all our pain and grief to You as we release our children to Your care. Thank You for continuing to be there to take us from the valley to the mountaintop. We gladly take off our sackcloth and ask You to wash away the ashes as You turn our mourning into dancing. I pray in Jesus Name. Amen.*

About the Author

Charlotte holds a Bachelor's degree in English and a Master's in Special Education. After teaching public school for 30 years, she retired to teach and write for Him. Upon retirement, she taught a women's Bible study for five years, using Kay Arthur's *Precept Upon Precept* studies. Then the Lord prompted her to write full time. She loves the Lord with all her heart and wants to share that love with others. For a number of years, Charlotte gave books to others to read of God's love; finally, she decided to write some of my own. Her main passion is to spread the gospel message. She believes through writing she can reach more people than by any other method. She enjoys the process of writing and feels the Master's pleasure when she writes. Her purpose in life is to please Him. Like Jeremiah, His word and message is like fire in her bones. She cannot be silent. She likes to write across the genres: nonfiction, fiction, poetry, devotionals, articles, short stories, and songs. Recently, she went back to leading Bible study as well. She also loves to speak, especially to groups of women. She lives in northwest Houston with her husband of 32 years. Charles owns and operates North Houston Exterminators.

AFFILIATIONS/ORGANIZATIONS:

ACFW (American Christian Fiction Writers)

CWGI (Christian Writers Group International)

IWA! (Inspirational Writers Alive!)

WOTS (Writers On the Storm) local ACFW

Humble Retired Teachers Association

Glorieta Christian Writers Conference Alumni

Mount Hermon Writers Conference Alumni

Delaware Christian Writers Conference Alumni

Colorado Christian Writers Conference Alumni

Greater Philadelphia Christian Writers Conference Alumni

Sandy Cove Christian Writers Conference Alumni

ACFW Conference Alumni

Blue Ridge Christian Writers Conference Alumni

A Sample of published works with release dates

NON-FICTION BOOKS

Praise the Lord for Roaches! (Publish America/December 2002)

Inspirations Book of Anthology (Hurley House Publishing/Dec. 2004)

Trusting Him In Your Grief/Charlotte Holt

Contributor for *I Must Decrease* by Janice Thompson
(Barbour 2005)

Contributor for *Memories of Mothers (Xulon Press
2007) Multi-Colored Love*

Contributor for *Miracles and Rescues* (Guideposts
Books 2007) *God Comforts the Broken Heart*

Contributor for *Miracles and Nature* (Guideposts Books
2008) *Asleep in the Boat*

Contributor for *A Scrapbook of Christmas First*
(Leafwood Publishers 2008) *Waffle House*

Contributor for *Secrets to Parenting your Adult Child*
(Bethany House 2011) *Handle Disappoints with Care*

Contributor for *Hurray God!* (Wine Press Publishing
2011) *Prayer Confirmation*

ARTICLES:

A Model for Sunday School
(**http://sundayschool.ag.org/ 2004**)

Trusting Him In Your Grief/Charlotte Holt

Dreams Come True: 7 Keys to Publication
(http://spiritledwriter.com. /**June 2004**)

Come Home, It's Suppertime (**Nostalgia Magazine**
/**August 2004**)

Mistletoe Madness
(www.americanchristianfictionwriters.com /**December
2005**)

Hawaii in Texas (www.bestplaceshawaii.com /**February
2006**)

Turn a Frog into a Prince (Living Magazine /**Spring
2007**)

Ten Essential 'E's for Writers (http://spiritledwriter.com
/**March 2007**)

Easter Celebration
(http://www.humblewms.blogspot.com/ **April 2009**)
The Exchange (Teachers of Vision Magazine/ **Winter
2012**)

Endorsement

Trusting Him in Your Grief will resonate deeply with parents who have lost a child. This tender, uplifting collection of true stories will offer grieving parents the chance to trust the Lord, even in the midst of their pain. Charlotte Holt has done a marvelous job of weaving together true vignettes of life and loss while sharing God's undying message of hope for the future. - Janice Thompson, author of *Parenting Teens: A Field Guide* and many other books, fiction and nonfiction.

Janice A. Thompson
"Scaling Heights, Lifting Hearts"
www.janiceathompson.com

4980198R00162

Printed in Great Britain
by Amazon.co.uk, Ltd.,
Marston Gate.